The Diaries of

A Collection of True Short Stories

By STU ARMSTRONG

ISBN-13: 978-1495908316   ISBN-10: 1495908313

Copyright © 2014 Stu Armstrong all rights reserved.

2nd Edition.

(First Published December 2013 © Stu Armstrong)

Find us on Facebook at **facebook.com/bookdoorman**

Find us on the web at **www.stuarmstrong.com**

No part of this book may be copied or reproduced in any way shape or form without the express permission of the Author.

This book is based on some true events, however, has been fictionalized and all persons & places & incidents appearing in this work are fictitious. Any resemblance to real places, Incidents real people, living or dead, is entirely coincidental & no responsibility will be accepted by the Author. Names have been changed to protect the innocent & the Guilty.

©Stu Armstrong 2014.

Stu Armstrong

"Last night when I finished my shift all I wanted to do was go home and sleep, but on the way I chased and caught a man that had stolen a woman's handbag and reunited her with it, she was so drunk she didn't know where she was, I made sure that she was safe and put her into a taxi to get her home. Just as I was near to my car I saw three lads beating the living shit out of one lad, I chased them of and checked he was ok............................

I bet you don't see that on YouTube!"

Gary Coombes

"Sometimes in life, the only thing that you can do to

The Diaries of a Doorman

combat violence is to use a greater proportion of violence, with some people it's all that they understand"

Un-Named North East Door Legend

> How many Doorman does it take to push someone down the stairs? Non, he fell!

Above: My favorite joke (It's not like that these days)

When I published the first edition of this book a week before Christmas 2013 I was in for a shock, I never ever thought that my book would take off the way it did. On the first day it sold 30 copies and I was pleased with that, on the second it just took off and the third I just went through the roof! Then I waited for the feedback and the comments, a little apprehensively granted, but I had now reason to worry, the comments coming to the Facebook page were all amazing and the Amazon reviews all 5 Star ratings and fantastic comments.

I am now working on a second book which was never the plan, so many people have asked me to write a second one as they loved the first one so much that I can hardly refuse. So to all of you who bought the first edition of my book 'The Diaries of a Doorman – A Collection of True Short Stories' Thank you! You have inspired the follow-up book that is due for release in early spring 2014.

Stu Armstrong

Dedication

The Diaries of a Doorman

I have to dedicate this book to an amazing strong woman who played a huge part in my life, the person that made me believe that if I want something enough then there is nothing in the world that I can't achieve. She would often be heard talking to her TV saying "And they get bloody paid for that? Our Stuart could do that" Well here I am doing it.

This book is dedicated to the memory of a very special lady, Jean Malcolm Stewart Armstrong, my Granny, always in my heart, and also to Nicki, the best thing that I ever lost!

Acknowledgments

Ever since I was a child I have wanted to write a book. Many times I have started, stopped and then given up. So finally here it is, partly thanks to some encouragement and words of wisdom from published authors and friends of mine Robin Barrett www.robin-barratt.com and Steve Wraith www.wraithpromotions.com. Thanks Lads!
My book is for all of the Armstrong's in my life, those that are living and also those who have moved on to a better place. You have all played a special part in my life, Especially Ben, Luca and Sol.

As this book is being self-published on a zero budget I spent a lot of time thinking of each one of my friends to proofread for me, each time I came back to the same person so a huge heartfelt thanks go out to Kristie Cole. Scott Telfer what can I say, thanks so much for your work and skill producing the covers and other artwork for me.

Thank you so much to my 12 years old Son, Ben, for taking the front cover photograph, and last but not least, Dan Chapman thanks for humouring for the past six months and listening to these stories, over and over and over again!

I would also like to say a big thank you for all of the help and support that I have had from the members of my online forum 'UK Bouncers'.

Top bunch of people & top banter, long may it stay the biggest & best group of its kind.
www.ukbouncers.com

If I don't say something about these lot I will never hear to end of it, they have done bog all for this book but there my good friends so a big thanks to some very good friends!

"The Sima Lads"

One last note to all of you Bouncers, Doorman, Door Supervisors or whatever the fuck you want to call yourself out there.

"Have a safe one and make it home in one piece!"

Contents

Acknowledgments 6
A WORD FROM THE AUTHOR 10
FOREWORD BY ROBIN BARRATT 12
CHAPTER ONE 14
  The Scotsmen, the Palm Tree, the Shot Girl and the Flood. 14
CHAPTER TWO 21
  The Working Men's Club. 21
CHAPTER THREE 26
  First Night on the Door. 26
CHAPTER FOUR 33
  The Disappearing Doorman. 33
CHAPTER FIVE 37
  Classy Ladies. 37
CHAPTER SIX 40
  Ginger Powers 40
CHAPTER SEVEN 47
  Life Savers 47
CHAPTER EIGHT 54
  THE HORSE SHOE BAR 54
CHAPTER NINE 65
  Basque Attack 65
CHAPTER TEN 68
  Following in my Father's footsteps? 68
CHAPTER ELEVEN 72
  Bit of a Let-down 72
CHAPTER TWELVE 77
  The 'Goodfellas' Party 77
CHAPTER THIRTEEN 82

Bouncing in the Sun 82

CHAPTER FOURTEEN **104**
The Good, The Bad & the Sad – Written by Ivan 'Doc' Holiday 104

CHAPTER FIFETEEN **108**
Bouncer the Movie 108

CHAPTER SIXTEEN **110**
Channel 4's 'Bouncers' 110

CHAPTER 17 .... **116**
So, You want to be a Bouncer? 116

ABOUT THE AUTHOR **117**

Stu Armstrong

A Word from the Author

I hope that you enjoy my book. This is my first book it's something that I have always wanted to do, and I would like to make it clear from the outset that I have not written this book to claim that I am the world's best Doorman, to play the big 'I am'. I have also not written this book to play the hard man, like many other Bouncers have done in the past with theirs.

To the piss takers out there, and I am sure there will many. I just want to say, I don't care what you think, I wanted to write a book and become published and I have. Simple as that!

Being a Doorman is a job, nothing more, nothing less, sometimes good, very often not so good. I do the job, but I don't live the so called Bouncers life style, which to be honest I think has pretty much died off. It's just a job like any other.

Yeah sure, it can be dangerous and yes, you can get hurt, which I have been on more than one occasion. But you can also get bored, cold, tired and sometimes totally fed up, and it also screws up relationships and impedes on family time and that is the worst thing in the world.

So just remember next time you have a night out that the Bouncers are no different to you. They are doing their job, most likely for their families, just the same as you. So say hello, show some respect and I guarantee that you will get the same back. My way, right it wrong is to treat people with respect. Show some respect and nine times out of ten you will be given respect back.

Just think for a moment, would you like to do our job? Could you do our job? Standing around in the cold, rain, sleet and snow, yet still opening the door for you. Greeting you with a smile. Still poised ready to see who wants to take a crack at you tonight. The quietest nights are the worst, the most boring and the most tiring. Standing there for hours with your brain and body ready to react within a fraction of a second, to god only knows what.

So could you do it? Would you do it? Remember if it wasn't for the excellent Door staff in this country, then bars, clubs and anywhere else that sell alcohol would be nothing but anarchy! We make pubs, clubs, nightclubs and all other kinds of venues safe for you to enjoy. So next time you see some horror video of a Bouncer online just ask yourself, is this the whole story that I can see? Did something happen beforehand? Just what was the catalyst? It's human nature just to go for the action shots but they don't give you the full picture of the incident. So next time you see something like this then please give that a thought.

Yeah, I can be a complete bastard I suppose, if I have to be, but I am only a bastard to bastards. Show me respect I will give the same back, don't and I won't. Simple. So for whatever reason you are asked to leave a venue then just leave the venue, you don't need the grief and sure as hell the doorman doesn't either! No doubt he has had grief all night and will get even more later on. I have written this book because all of my life I have had a love of books, of reading and of the written world. So here it is. Good, bad or ugly this is my book. Hope that you enjoy it!

Stu Armstrong

Stu Armstrong

Foreword by Robin Barratt

I am asked a lot about what working the **doors was** like back in the '80s and '90s compared to now. I always say how different the doors were; how it was a much more violent world, with a lot less accountability. We could fight when we wanted and do what we wanted, or indeed needed, with relative impunity.

Doormen were rarely arrested and venue managers expected a fighter on the doors, as did of course, the door team. No one would ever employ you without being able to mix-it with the best.

This aspect of working the doors has changed immeasurably. In today's world few managers would ever employ a real fighter and if a door supervisor hit someone on today's doors, there would be a good chance of him or her getting arrested, and thus probably thereafter sacked.

Door-staff now of course need an SIA license to work, which was brought into the industry with the intention of professionalising it, but had the complete opposite effect. With the commercialisation of the door supervisor training course and guaranteed pass rates, anyone and everyone can get a license and work the doors, regardless of your background or ability. Indeed, door supervisor training courses are one of the first things the Government puts Job Seekers on to get the unemployed out of work, and yet, ironically, punters haven't changed one bit, they are still as violent as ever (perhaps even more violent). When they have had a few too many, they are rude, nasty and have little respect, long gone are the days when punters respected doorstaff.

Punters know they can get away with almost anything and there is now very little doorstaff can do. I am of the old school; if someone does something wrong then teach them a lesson, and it is sure that they will never do it again. Now, punters can do what they want, whenever they want because they are never taught otherwise. Even in the door supervisor training courses, students are taught not to put themselves in harm's way. Really!

So the doors have changed, but the punters haven't. Saying that though, there are of course many excellent door staff that really do take pride in their work and whose priority is to make the venue safe for their customers.

The doors are still a wild, unusual and often bizarre world, animated with characters and situations that defy belief, some of which you can read here in Stu's book of door stories. Often scary, occasionally funny, Stu's book will certainly entertain you and have you wonder at what life is like when the sun sets and the doormen and punters go out to play! Enjoy!

Robin Barratt

Former Doorman, Author & Writer of

'Tough Talk' Magazine   www.robin-barratt.com

Stu Armstrong

CHAPTER ONE

The Scotsmen, the Palm Tree, the Shot Girl and the Flood.

It was a Friday Night in the middle of August, a good few years ago now. I started the shift along with another lad and it seemed like another unremarkable, normal night. As always, I sent the other lad to the door and I did what has always been my thing; walk around the bar, check the fire exits, a quick toilet check, but most importantly, a customer check.

This was followed by a bit of crack with some of the regulars and a quick laugh or joke with some out of towners to get a bit of rapport going ready for the night's antics. Then off to the door to get on with the job, as you do. It was a busy night, with around 300 punters in a venue that will hold around 350, a pretty standard night back in the day.

There were mainly regulars at this point. Mixed with a couple of small groups and a couple of large Hen parties mixed with the usual smattering of Scotsmen who seem to get everywhere, so all in all it looked set for a pretty standard night.

Now this was a decent venue, but like all bars and clubs in this day and age we had to be on the lookout for drug abuse. Its wasn't commonplace in this particular bar, but on the other hand, if I had a pound for all those that I have caught having cheeky line, well you know the rest. As a matter of standard practice, we do something which most Doormen do; regular toilet checks. I sent the other Doorman downstairs to the toilets and no sooner had he left. I got a radio call came through for assistance. So down I went like a startled gazelle with all the grace of the Ark Royal, and sure enough he had caught two Scottish Lads having a cheeky line. As per the rules of the venue they were both searched and neither of them had anything on them, maybe half of Columbia up their noses but nothing left on them. Following our normal procedures we began to eject them from the venue.

Now, a thing I have always believed in and I still believe to this day, is that anyone who needs to be ejected, should always be ejected straight out of the closest exit or fire exit. So the first bloke that was with the other Doorman, calm and meek as a mouse, walked out with no resistance given. He went down the stairs from the gents and straight out of the fire exit as directed. So what about the other one? Well lucky me I got the 'wannabe' fighter. He had decided he didn't want to go. He chucked a punch which was deflected and he was grabbed and promptly marched out, or as we like to say in the North East, 'ragged out'. I then went straight on the radio to let the other bars and Police know what had happened, followed by a description of the lads. Pretty standard up to now yeah? Well this is where it starts to get interesting.....

We went back to the front door and by now we had a lot of Scottish lads milling around just inside the bar. One of them got a phone call and looked straight at me. Instantly I thought 'Here we go, Mr Wannabe must be on the phone to him' and oh how right I was. The Telephone guy came over to me and started the usual, "Why did you chuck my two pals out? "We have just come to meet them?"" With bit of a stance on him and a bit of an attitude, he had about ten of his mates standing behind him, and me with one mate standing next me. So I said to him, '"Mate, come over here and lets have a crack on". So he came with me and I explained what had happened and I added '… "To be honest mate they did ok for themselves, they didn't get caught with any gear, your pal that threw a punch wasn't hurt and they have both been chucked out the bar, simple as".

So the bloke though about it and said "Oh well, you can't take them Wankers anywhere", but still with that certain something about him that kept me on my toes and ready. A few minutes later he came back and started again, with the standard "Do you know who I am" to which my reply has always been "Well if you don't know mate how I am meant to?" He came with his mates behind him, like following the pied piper and started to get aggressive, so I turned to the mouth piece and said "Look mate, your pals got caught snorting Coke, they have been chucked out, you and your mates obviously have a problem with that, fair enough. But I am doing my job and if they didn't want chucked out they shouldn't be doing drugs in my bar".

By now we were at a bit of a stand-off. Two against ten, so I said, "Look lads finish your drinks and get yourselves to another bar, you're not getting served here again". Just at that moment I saw one of the older fella's who drinks in the bar, hobble off with his stick out of my peripheral vision and I knew where he was going. Over the next few minutes or so the lads got more and more aggressive and their stances and tones changed. At that point I knew what to expect. Just then the two lads that run the door on the bar up the street came walking down into my bar, thanks to the old bloke. The Scotsmen started and all hell was let loose, punches flying the lot. I managed to get hold of Mr Mouthpiece, who was a big old lump, in a Nelson and began dragging him out. What the hell happened to me next I don't know but he somehow flipped me and next thing I knew I was on the ground with Mr Mouthpiece and his mate punching and kicking me.

At this point I was throwing punches as hard and fast as I could. The pub manager, unbeknown to me, was running over to help, not really knowing what to do, but his heart was in the right place. He ran over and grabbed my right hand, trying to pull me up. Meanwhile the blows from Mr Mouthpiece and his mate were still reigning down on me.

Well what happened next couldn't have been avoided. I still had a left hand and I had no choice but to throw a left hook at the manager to get him off my hand. I honestly didn't know it was the manager! I then somehow got one of the Scottish lads off me with a combination of punches and kicks, but Mr Mouthpiece still wouldn't give up. I managed to get half way up but he still had the massive advantage of both position and size. All of a sudden a customer, who as it happens was an ex Doorman, ran over and swiped Mr Mouthpiece totally poleaxing him, and then sat on him. He shouted over to me "Go on then lad, get stuck in and have fun I will hold this fucker for you".

The Diaries of a Doorman

I saw at the other side of the bar the lad who worked for me pinned to the floor. I ran over and got the aggressor in a choke hold, pulled him backwards and applied just the right amount of pressure to safely put him to sleep.

I turned my attention to one of the lads from the bar up the street taking two more Scotsmen out in headlocks. He had one under each arm, with two more Scotsmen coming at him. Me and my mate ran at them and managed to drag them back, but there was one more Scotsman; he was a real mountain of a man. He ran from the double headlock melee. Just outside of the bar, as in many, there were some large heavy false palm trees. Well you can guess what the mountain man was going to do next...
He picked up one of the trees with sheer dumb strength and started to raise it as if to hit the bouncer with it. I could see this all unfolding before me but couldn't do anything as I was still fighting to get one of the nutters out.

I then saw out of the corner of my eye, like an avenging angel, something which is now local folklore, the shot girl from a bar round the corner was walking past on her way to work, and she stands at 5ft tall on a good day. She ran at the mountain man and somehow managed to latch herself around his neck. She was shouting "Don't think so mate" and punching him. She cracked him right in the face and made him drop the tree. This was an amazing sight to see.

Just then sirens started in the distance and some of the Scotsmen ran off shouting the usual threats. The police turned up and arrested those that were left. As one of them was getting man-handled into the back of the van he shouted "The other 50 lads will be here tomorrow, they will be in to see you'" to which I replied "Course mate looking forward to it, sleep well in your cell", thinking at the time it was just the usual crap.

The rest of the night then passed, as it sometimes does, uneventfully, apart from an interesting chat with the manager about the punch in the face that he received from me. Oh and the mountain of paperwork and incident logs, as is now the way. The next day arrived and it was a pretty standard sort of a Saturday. I woke up around 10am by the roar of my three sons, staggered down the stairs like something that had just left the swamp, and had bit of a chuckle to myself about the shot girl and the palm tree. I felt a bit achy, but not too worse for wear considering the previous night's antics.

So time marched on and after a good day with the kids, of I went for the three S's; Shit, Shower and Shave. I got my door clobber and boots on ready to see what the night would bring. Well was I in for a surprise, I tell you what, even after all the years on the door you just couldn't make up what that night was going to bring.

I was back at my regular venue again for a 9pm start and I walked into a packed, and I mean packed, bar for this time of night. I was ready to sign in and get radioed up and what not. As soon as I set foot inside the bar the most bizarre thing happened, I was more or less mobbed by Scotsmen. Rather than try and kick off as I had expected, they started taking my photograph with their phones, and I could hear someone saying "That looks like the Bastard there". Shocked I said "what the hell you playing at here lads?" The group was easily 40 to 50 strong. No answers were given and they walked off back to their respective tables, some in the beer garden and some in the bar.

Having at that point the old 'Bouncers Belly' feeling, I went into to the office with the other lad, signed in and got my radio on. I then went back into the bar along with the other Doorman. I heard one of the Scotsmen now saying "I have sent the photo over to see if it's him"". I knew exactly what the score was; it was the other 50 lads who were coming to the town today to meet the lads from last night. You know the ones that I considered to be figments of the imagination!

As I was having a quick word with the other Doorman about the best course of action, five policemen started walking down the beer garden towards the door. The Scotsmen instantly started drifting out. The Police were there purely and simply for what I term 'A Walk About', which considered normal in a busy area is populated by bars and clubs. They tend to wander through the bar, checking numbers, faces etc. It's often a good help to us, as anyone that is up to no-good, no matter if we are aware or not, usually just drift out.

Before I could even mention my new found stardom to one of the Policemen, the Scotsmen had all downed their pints and bottles and left, the rest of the night passed without any further problems, but I was expecting some trouble from these Scottish lads at the end of the night. I had passed the word around the Door Staff at other venues and a few times over the night I heard radio calls to the police about fights and drug taking, which to be honest wasn't unusual back then. I was thinking to myself that it was my little friends again.

So the shift was over, paperwork was done and it was time to leave the bar. I was expecting a remake of Rob Roy to take place but all was quiet. Just as I was about to sign off the police radio I heard a call from the one and only hotel in the area, where unbeknown to me at the time all of these Scotsmen were staying, asking for the police to eject some guests for criminal damage.

Anyway we left the bar and started walking down the street to make our way home through past the Kebab and Pizza shop. We saw around 30 or 40 men walking up the street with sports bags and suitcases in hand. My Scottish friends from before, obviously just evicted from the hotel. One of them came up to me, slightly worse for the wear on drink and god knows what else. He didn't recognise me and said '"Here, Pal look at this." He showed me a video on his phone of them turning on all of the taps, filling up all sinks and baths and letting them overflow to flood the hotel. Obviously this was the criminal damage that I heard on the radio.

Anyway the bloke with the video on his phone still didn't recognise me and said, "Look I have £600 here in cash". He pulled out a big wad of cash, dropped a couple of wraps of what I presumed to be cocaine, and asked me if I could arrange a six seated taxi to take him and five of his friends back up North of the Border to Glasgow. This is when I had an idea to get a little revenge. "Yes mate no problem. Give me five minutes and I will arrange something" I said. The other Doorman, shocked, said "What are you doing? Let's just go before we get recognised". I knew that's what I should have done but I couldn't resist the sweet taste of revenge that I was beginning to taste in my mouth.

Now, all Doormen know a taxi driver that they can ring on their mobiles, that's just part of the game. I put a call in to a friend that happened to have a minibus that he used as a taxi and after a quick chat he was on his way to pick up some of my new found friends. I told him that they had the cash and he had to take the cash up front. When he got there they all piled aboard drinking bottles of lager and all kinds of other intoxicating stuff. I waited until they paid the driver and off he went with a twinkle in his eye.

Half an hour later I got the phone call I had been waiting for. It had me in hysterics. Just as I had suggested they might, with all they had been drinking, they were soon caught short. Just as the driver had drove as far as the A1. On a dark, quiet, desolated stretch of the A1 just north of Newcastle, the driver pulled into a lay-by. One by one they staggered off the minibus to relieve themselves in the bushes. The second the last one was off the minibus, you guessed it, the drivers foot was flat to the floor and off he flew up the A1 with the door still open, leaving them all with their mouths open and mid piss!

At the next lay-by he stopped, dumped the luggage and emptied bottles and a decent size bag of coke all over the ground and headed for home. We earned a three way split on the taxi fare for him, me and the other Doorman!

Sometimes you have just see how things pan out in this game and smile!

CHAPTER TWO

The Working Men's Club.

It was a Sunday afternoon on a winter's day in January. There was snow outside and it was colder than a snowman's ice Lolly. I was at home with the wife and kids, lounging on the settee watching TV. 'This is the life' I thought to myself. Just then my phone warbled out a text message. It was from an old mate of mine. He was asking if I would do him a favour and cover a shift at a working men's club, I really couldn't be arsed but he went on and on at me, and after all if you can help a mate out and all that!

Anyone that knows the area that this place was in would soon tell you that it's not in exactly what you could call the most salubrious of areas, in fact a lot of people would have preferred to jump of a cliff rather than work here, but what the hell, I said I would do it. I looked out of the window just to double check the snow wasn't too bad for the journey. This was at about 2pm and my shift was due to start at 8pm, so plenty time.

So I went about the afternoon as usual. The best afternoons are always when it's cold outside and you're inside with your family in the warm just relaxing. As the early darkness began to enclose the street, I close the curtains to shut the cold out and at about 7pm I started getting ready for work; thermal socks, black boots, black trousers, white shirt, black tie and in this weather most definitely my black coat. I kissed the family goodbye and opened the front door only to be greeted with 2ft of snow! Bloody great! Especially since at the time I was driving a rear wheel car.

So off I went, spade in the boot (I keep a spade in the boot for a reason you know), and a couple of bags of sand. After about an hour of terrible conditions I eventually arrived, a lot more than a few minutes late. I took one look at the place and thought to myself 'Oh for fucks sake, my car won't even be here when I come back, and if it is it will be up on bloody bricks'.

The social club itself was a big place, with steel shutters on most of the windows and adorned with graffiti. It looked dwarfed by the huge block of flats standing directly behind it, they have been massively improved these days but at the time it just looked like 13 stories of squalor, this really was bandit country. 'Well here goes' I said to myself as I walked up the stairs to the entrance and what did I find? Only weirdest door I have ever been on that's what, heavy glass doors that stayed permanently closed unless a button was pressed from inside or a member swiped their card on the way in.

I knocked and a friendly faced doorman looked out and opened the door for me. I went in and found a doorman in his mid 50's, balding with a red ruddy face, a bloke called Charlie, who I was later to become friends with for a while, that was until I learned that he was a man of many personalities and even more lies! Charlie showed me around and took me down into a dubious looking cellar where I swear the sacrifice goats and vestal virgins but no such luck only goats when I get there! No seriously, no goats or virgins in fact I think there wouldn't have been any virgins round these parts since before the war. This was the inner sanctum, this was the committee room, and it really was like the inner sanctum of a religious cult.

So I sign the book and then back to the door to start work. When asking about the odd door I was told that the doors were in fact Bullet proof due to the last doorman being shot whilst on duty! (As I got to know Charlie later I am not exactly sure that he was telling the truth) Nice place I thought. Now this place has two rooms, the bar and the lounge. Women under no circumstances were permitted into the bar area and only to the lounge or concert room as they called it. God forbid that a female ever set foot in the Holy Grail that was the bar! Except to serve the beer and clean up obviously.

Charlie gave me the rundown on what to expect, he said that there was one bloke in the bar area that was so pissed that he had actually shit himself, with a look of disgust I said "Come on then we had better sling him out"', to which I got the quick reply "Don't be a fucking idiot, that's the chair of the committee"!

The Diaries of a Doorman

As the night went on I became a dab hand with the button press on the door. Charlie turned to me and said "Do you smoke mate? Why not nip out for a quick tab" I thought well why not, a quick one won't harm. Charlie told me just to stand out front, down the steps and to the side to smoke. Off I went lighting my cigarette and watching the smoke in the cold night air spiralling away towards the 12 stories of hell. It then struck me. If we have to stand behind bullet proof glass doors as the last Doorman got shot then… "SHIT", I finished my tab in record time and went back inside I can tell you!

By then, people were starting to fill up the concert room for the bingo, Charlie turned to me and told me that this was where his Special Forces background came in handy, to which I laughed only to be met with a stony face from Charlie. "Are you for real mate, you use Special Forces training in the bingo room?" I said, to which he nodded his head and cracked his knuckles. 'We've got a right one here' I think to myself, and it turned out to be right'!

Anyway half an hour later while Charlie was doing some toilet checks, or so he said. I was called into the bingo room to see about two hundred geriatrics waving their walking sticks and effing and blinding at a lad in his 20's. The lad was a big lump, with his trademark 'Tap out' t-shirt stretched over his steroid filled arms. He was on top of the bingo caller throwing down punches more animated than damage causing, I remember thinking to myself as I dodged the bottles and glasses that were being thrown by the old farts and the direction of the bother.

So I ran over, put him in a Nelson and dragged him, kicking and screaming out of the concert room towards the front door. As I moved near to the doors there was Charlie, my so called 'Brother in Arms' standing there with a stupid look on his face drinking a cup of tea. I did expect Charlie to open the doors and give me a hand but he just looked at me and said "what are doing?"" To which I replied in a rather pissed off tone "Riding my fucking bike action man what do you think"? I am slinging this overgrown monkey fucker out". Charlie then said, with all seriousness "No, you can't chuck him out, his dad and his granddad are on the committee just hold him there until one of the committee men comes out" and much to my disbelief he then dug a custard cream out of his pocket and dipped it in his tea while I was still struggling with 'Tap Out Boy'.

Just then one of the committee came out of the concert room and said "Let him go then lad". "You have got to be kidding, really, do you know what he has just done?" I said. He took a long slow look at me and replied "It's only young Steve, Dan's boy, just high spirits, let him go and he can go back in the bar". I couldn't quite believe my ears but really didn't have a choice and when I let him go what a smug bastard he was, and off he scurried back into the bar. That's bloody committee men for you.

Most of the shift passed by pretty uneventful with more of Charlie's weird and unbelievable stories. Everything from jumping out of planes to sailing the high seas looking for pirates, and oh about him being a survival expert and how he could eat, drink, wipe his arse and no doubt make a helicopter, from berries!

Just about half an hour from the end of the shift a woman in her mid-forties came running out of the concert room; her makeup applied by polyfilla and a trowel with the waft of cheap sickly perfume trailing behind her. She also had no shoes on. She was screaming "He has done it again the dirty bastard, he has done it again", I asked who had done what and she told me that old Bobby had a shoe fetish and had nicked her red patent leather high heels. "Why the hell would he do that?" I asked, to which the woman replied "go into the gents and you will find out!"

So to be honest a little apprehensively, worried about what the hell I might find off I went into the gents with Charlie still munching away on his biscuits. When I got in there all of the traps were empty apart from one. The stalls were only around 5ft high, the tops being chopped off in a bid to stop drug use in the club, well I presume that's what the doors had been butchered for anyway. I could hear heaving breathing and grunting and knew before I looked that whatever was going in there, I didn't want to see. Anyway I poked my head over the top of the cubicle door only to see the most disgusting sight that I have seen in my life!

The Diaries of a Doorman

There was old Bobby sitting there with his pants around his ankles, and his cock in his hand, wanking off into one of the shoes! "Dirty dirty bastard!!! Well committee or no committee this sick pervert was booted out, after I put my gloves on that was! At the end of that shift, much to my relief, my car was still there, unlocking it and climbing into the driver's seat I saw a group of figures moving quickly in the shadows across the frozen snowy car park, "There's that bastard that chucked old wanky out" I heard one women shout and as they emerged from the shadows there was a lynch mob hunting me down, there must have been a good ten or some old women ranting and raving their way towards me led by, who I later found out, Old Bobby's wife, or "Old Wanky" as she called him. Well it was like a cross between whacky races and Bambi on ice, but somehow I managed to get my car out of the car park, almost crying with laughter as I did so.

CHAPTER THREE

First Night on the Door

Over the years, ever since I began in the pub trade I have always ended up 'Doing the Door', just as and when I was needed, either in my own pubs, down the local or in friend's bars and clubs, or as a favour if something kicked off. But here I was about to work the door in an official capacity, for the very first time. You need to remember that back in the day; this was way before the SIA, or even the council badges and the training. Training in this respect just wasn't existent; in fact really the only qualification was that you were able to 'Have a Ruck'. I would be a liar if I said that I wasn't even a little bit nervous, it was a somewhat daunting idea. It was different to managing my own bars as I often had doormen working for me and would only jump into the mêlée if they needed me.

I was an old-school pub manager that would be serving one second and vaulting the bar to break up a fight the next. Or I would jump up and break stuff up in my local if things kicked off, which they often did in my local back then. But all of that was very different indeed, it wasn't your main focus, it wasn't your reason for being there. As a manager or a punter it would just go 'BOOM', the trouble would start, the adrenaline would kick in, and without thinking you would be straight in there.

But this was different, you were waiting for trouble. You were the sheriff so to speak, the buck started and stopped with you. All of these questions and doubts filled my mind as I was getting ready, what if I can't handle it? What if I ended up in hospital? But worst of all, what if I bottled out? How could I live with myself then? What if this, what if that, what if the other? A thousand reasons why I shouldn't be doing this filled my mind at 100mph. The venue that I was working I knew well. I went under two names and I really can't remember if it was Wharfs of The Waterfront at the time, a venue set over three floors on the Fish Quay in my home town of North

The Diaries of a Doorman

Shields, a fishing town set on the banks of the river Tyne. I knew the management, I knew the staff, I knew the regulars and I knew the locals. The ground and first floor were regular bars, with a slight touch of the pompous 'Real Ale Trail', strived for but not quite achieved.

You know the kind of places I mean; you still see hundreds of them like that to this day, up and down the country. The third floor oddly enough was an Italian restaurant. So what could be so bad about that then? It wasn't like there was ever any trouble, or like it even got busy, that is apart from May Bank Holiday Weekend when 'The Fish Quay Festival' was held. Originally called 'The Fisherman's Regatta', it was a small celebration for Fishermen who sailed out to the North Sea to find their pots of gold from the river Tyne.

As the son of a onetime trawler man this was one of the highlights of the year when I was young. All of the boats would be dressed up with homemade flags and bunting and a carnival type atmosphere adorned North Shields for this one day of the year, with the highlight being the blessing of the fleet when all of the boats from the North Shields fleet decorated in all the colours of the rainbow would slowly perform a watery procession up the Tyne.

I will never forget the day that my Dad's boat won best decorated of the fleet with the best set of flagging anyone had seen. In comparison to the homemade tat on the other boats this boat really stood out from the rest, rigged from masts to wheelhouse and all around the guard rails with a set of manufactured expensive rigged flags. The very same flags that my Mother had borrowed for the occasion from a local petrol station and car dealership!

Anyway as with most things nowadays, of big businesses and corporate sponsorships, the local council jumped on the bandwagon and as far as I am concerned, ruined the regatta. It turned this one traditional day for fishermen, families and locals into a three day 'Fish Quay Festival'.

During these three days in May, it isn't a place for the feint hearted after about 1pm. From around 10am all the bars along 'the Quay' would open, along with the many stalls and fairground rides, and it wasn't bad at all if you were there early doors. A lot of families and those with young children would go down early, enjoy the stalls, the rides and more often than not some of the tat, then get some chips and walk back up the steep bank to North Shields. But at about 1pm the people that had been drinking since 10am, or in the case of an old fisherman's bar 'The Bottom Dolphin' that opened early, from 6am every day, people were very drunk. The acts at the so called music festival would start on the live stage, just across the road from the Waterfront, and this became a heady mix for some, even that early in the day. Too much alcohol, fairground rides and music…

So, I was all dressed and ready for my first shift on the door. I started at 11am, and when I asked what time we finished when it took the three day job it was told, just when they closed. I checked myself in the mirror, did I look that part? Well after some self-criticism yeah, I think I did! Suited and booted with a black shirt, a black tie, a black coat for later on and a pair of black leather gloves, I was ready to go.

From where I lived at the time, I literally had to walk no more than ten yards and look over some black iron railings that had seen better days, to be able to see all the way down the very steep hill that led to the Fish Quay. I apprehensively walked over to take a look and it was quite busy already, this was at about 10.40am. So I began walking down the famous, and bloody steep, stag Line stairs that joined the old stag line building, now the Registry Office, to the Fish Quay.

When I was about halfway down the stairs, it felt like I was walking through a door, all of a sudden the noise, the shouts, the laughter, the noise of the fairground rides, the music and the smell of candy floss and fried onions. 'Well this is it!' I thought. Down the stairs I went and turned left for the 300 yard walk to the Waterfront to meet the lad I was working with, who was an experienced Doorman.

I was told that he would be there early, well before me, to discuss with the manager the finer points of looking after his bar during the madness that was the Fish Quay Festival. I got there at about

The Diaries of a Doorman

10.50pm and walked into the half empty bar. I couldn't see that lad that I was meant to be working for, so I approached the bar and asked the manager where he was and he said "OH, one of you has decided to turn up then have you?", to which I replied "I was told to start at 11am and the other lad who I am working for was meeting me here", he said his was coming down earlier than me to talk to you". Anyway he hadn't turned up, so the manager went through what he wanted, and I set to work thinking that he would be along in minute.

Just as I start walking to stand on the door the manager shouted me back "Stu!... Haven't you forgotten something?" I thought quickly, and rather nervously, to myself, 'what have I missed, what have I missed?" I racked my brains in that split second and my answer came out "No, mate I don't think I have". I walked back to the bar where he handed me a pint of lager. I stuck my hand out and took it, thinking that he wanted me to give it to someone, and said "Who's this for then?" , "You!" he said, "just shout every time you're ready for a refill'".

Now I know back in the day it was the norm for lads to have the odd pint on the door, but I had at least a 12 hour shift ahead so I said "Thanks Tom, but I would much rather have a cup of tea mate". "No worries mate" Tom said "get your pint down you while I put the kettle on". So off I went to the door, not even 11am, pint in hand, by myself. 'Hmm great start this is!' I thought.
Now because of trouble over the last few years all the bars had to use plastic glasses over the festival weekend, so I see an old local colourful character, Willie Telford walking past. Willie back then had a lot of problems, he was an alcoholic and spent most of his days from god knows where finding old couches and dragging them to outside the Mariners Arms, My aunt's old pub, where he would sit and drink most of the day, so as he walks past I shouted him over and gave him the pint, complete with plastic glass. He could hardly believe his luck.

So there I was, standing on the door for the very first time, dropped in the shit for the very first time. Shame it wasn't to be the last. It was an extremely busy day, absolutely rammed with people by lunchtime, still by myself I was fighting a losing battle. Or so I thought at the time, but looking back I suppose I did ok. 2pm came and so does the other lad, the one I was meant to be working with. He strolled up without a care in the world. I was fuming at him "Where the fuck were you?" I asked furiously, almost spitting venom with each word.

"Oh, err I was working" he said. "Working where"? At the bottom of a pint glass?" I spat as he was clearly half cut. So he started work. Then came the first chuck out of the day, a man in his forties who was stotting drunk. He was up on the second floor and I found him while 'going walk about' checking each of the bars. He was slumped in the corner by himself so I managed to stand him up and walk him out of the bar and onto the stairwell. Then I began helping him down the stairs. Just as he got to the bottom of the stairs he started kicking off. I was expecting my so called Head Doorman to give me a hand, I soon found my expectations were very wrong. He just stood there and watched.

I soon managed to get him in a full nelson and put him out of the bar. He was standing outside on the fish quay when he started telling us he would be back, he was going to get all of his mates and come back and 'give us something'. I suppose that being my first ever time on the door maybe I should have been a little wary, but to me you could just tell this bloke couldn't fight his way out a paper bag and was utterly full of shit.

What surprised me at this point was that the bloke I was working with, who was supposed to be a seasoned doorman, was shitting himself. He had absolute terror on his face. I told him to sober up and man up and went back to work. About an hour later I heard 'Mr King of Doorman' shouting "Stu, Stu quick he has come back with his mates!" I ran down from the upstairs bar taking the stairs two or three at a time. This was the first time that I had experienced an adrenaline rush on the door, and I liked it!

When I got to the foot of the stairs I shouted "where are they then?!" I was ready for battle I suppose, not knowing what to expect, but up for it never the less. "Over there getting served at the bar" came the reply. I couldn't believe my ears. He had let him back in. "At the fucking bar? You clown, why the fuck did you let him back in the bar?!" to which the reply came "Well there are three of them I didn't want to say no to them"

Just then the same bloke came over with his two mates behind him, strutting across the bar like 'Reservoir Puppies', you know the sort, all the gear and no idea. The bloke that I had put out was holding a hand behind his back and shouted to me "I have got something for you just like I promised!" So there I was, first time on the door, with a bloke who was half cut and as far as I was concerned had no idea and even less bottle. Along with three blokes, walking slowly towards me, one with something behind his back. 'What the hell was it? A knife, a bottle, a glass?'' I thought. I remember thinking of the plastic glass only rule and I felt a little better, but still all kinds of things were flying through my head once more, 'what if it's a gun?'

I was, and I don't mind telling you, starting to get very worried, scared if you like. I knew I had a lot to learn in this job, I knew that I was new to it and lacked experience. Even more so, I knew I was on my own as the gob shite that I was working with was going to do nothing to help me. He was standing there with his gob open like he was catching flies!

I wasn't really sure what to do. This is what they call a 'Flight of Fight situation' where instinct takes over and you either run away or you stand and fight. I had read a lot about this years earlier in phycology and I strongly believed that it was one of man's most primal instincts and was more or less out of your control. It's something deep within you, in your make up; who you are determines what you would do next.

Without thinking I called out to him "Stop where you are I want to see what the fuck your hiding behind you back, and I hope for your sake it's not some kind of weapon mate, because if it is I will take it off you and shove it up your arse!"' He looked at me with an odd look on his face, all I can really describe it as is a hurt look, like I had hurt his feelings which was the last thing that I expected. So slowly, he brought his hand out from behind his back, stammering all the while "I err, I err, I told you I would err, be back with a surprise" and in his hand I saw a glass, a glass of what looked like whiskey.

"What is that?" I asked him "What the hell are you playing at?" To which he replied "It's a surprise I have come back to buy you a whiskey to say sorry for being a dick" That really was the last thing that I expected, but it taught me a very valuable lesson on the door, always expect the unexpected, as it's always going to happen! Sometime good, sometimes bad, you just never can tell. More importantly, although this bloke was nothing he came to buy me a drink, it taught me to never ever underestimate anyone. To this day, a hell of a lot of years later, I still don't underestimate anyone, as you can just never tell.

....

And the thing is, I hate Whiskey!

CHAPTER FOUR

The Disappearing Doorman

This match was a funny old one for me, one of the few derby games that I wasn't working on the door. I got a phone call from my mate and fellow doorman Jimmy to say that his stepson Chris, also a doorman, was doing a Newcastle city centre door shift and finished at 3pm. It was now 5pm and Chris had made arrangements to go straight home for a family Sunday lunch but hadn't turned up, Jimmy asked if I had heard from him.

I had not, nor would I have expected to be honest! Jimmy was becoming worried but I just reassured him that Chris was a 20 year old grown man, he was only a couple of hours late home and that he would be fine and could look after himself. At 7pm the phone went again and Jimmy was now very worried. He said that Chris's phone was switched off and he just knew something terrible had happened to him after watching the TV News reports showing the level of violence. Jimmy told me that he was about to ring the police and report him missing, I thought that he was over reacting, but if it was one of my sons I suppose I would have felt the same. So to help, while Jimmy rang the police I started ringing round the hospitals, neither Police nor the Hospitals knew anything about him.

I was just starting to worry a little too, mainly because of the panic in Jimmy's voice. He told me that the police were coming round to see him and he asked if I would go up to his house. Well the Police are all well and good, but something that I have come to rely on over the years in times like this is the doorman's network. I posted some details and a photo of Chris on a local doorman's forum on Facebook and the response I received amazed me, it was simply staggering. Paul Rooks an old-school doorman, turned trainer rang me straight away "Stu if you want to go look for him my car is available", that was just one of the offers of help we had that night, the brotherhood really pulled together well that night.

So we jumped into the car and head of to where he was last working. I knew the other lads on the door and we had a bit crack on, but they said that he finished his shift hours ago and was mentioning that he was starving and was going straight home for his Sunday dinner that his mother was keeping warm. We checked a good few local bars, but nothing, not a bloody dickey bird, not a bloody sausage!! We headed back home and on the way I had an idea, an old mate of mine Louise was quite high up at the Metro, the Metro Is Tyneside's version of the London Underground just cleaner and without the rats. So I rang her and she said that she would issue a description around all staff by radio and email.

So we were sitting with a policeman giving him all of the details, but bugger me talk about slow, he was hardly what you would call lightning! Just then my phones went and it was Louise, my friend from the Metro "Stu we have found him and he is fine but absolutely mortal drunk"".

This was out of character for Chris, but what the hell he was safe. I drove up to Newcastle to collect him from the station and eventually I found him in the office having a cuppa with some of the staff. He was sprawled across a chair, door uniform, no tie or coat, which he later realised were lost, and his stab vest. My god what a mortal mess he really was! He started shouting and kicking off with me about his parents "I can't even go out and get pissed because my mother does this!" I couldn't help but laugh which seemed to calm things a bit. We thanked the Metro staff, who really had been amazing, and off went, at one point driving slowly out of Newcastle city centre, stop start in the traffic and I spotted a couple of absolute stunners with, as they do up here even in the winter, next to nothing on. "Dan, look at the plight of them" I said, he half looked and then shouted, "I don't even care" and put his head down almost to his lap, this made me roar with laughter and all I got from Chris was his trade mark phrase, "Fuck off Cunt"! Which made me laugh all the more.

It turned out that Chris had gone to a bar he has worked in a few times before, just for a swifty but ended up sat there and got himself that pissed that he lost his coat and tie and I dread to think what else, good job he wasn't in pink triangle, an area notoriously requested by gays or he may have lost more than he bargained for. But I think he had a good day, not that he can remember!

After the first edition of this book I was contacted by Steve Gallon, over Facebook, and believe it or not he was sitting reading the book and recognised himself as being part of this storey. Mike, an ex-Doorman was actually working on the Metro system this night and not only searched for 'The Disappearing Doorman', but he was also the one that found him!

Steve Gallon

Steve, the Hero of the storey added his comments:

"Well it had been a mad busy day being a derby match, and then all of a sudden I heard Louise putting a call out on the radio for everyone to be on the lookout for a male dressed in a Doorman uniform who had went missing. Well even though I was working as a ticker inspector I was also still on the Doors, so straight away it was my priority to find him, (the old brotherhood is still alive and well).

We were checking the stations and trains for a while keeping up to date with developments with Louise by radio, and then I spotted him looking all disorientated

I approached him and instantly recognised him as who we were looking for, he was mortal drunk but full of beans and I have got to say a really nice kid. I broke the ice by telling him a was a also a Doorman, which he seemed to have liked and then started telling me that he had worked a double shift for the football, he then mentioned a few doorman that he said he knew and was friends with, including Stu Armstrong, who I said that I also knew but by face only.

He went on to telling me that he had a few drinks but now just wanted to go home. We chatted and had a laugh for a while until we got the information over the radio that someone was coming to get him from the Central Station, so off on the metro we went having a good chat about working the doors. We got to Central Station and Stu Armstrong met us, who was very thankful for all of our help, and laughing at the plight of the drunken disappearing Doorman.

Myself and my supervisor Dean Burles and we were both really chuffed that me managed to help some fellow Doorman. So off you all went and we were straight back on duty! When we reported back to Louise smith, our manager, and gave her the good news she was pleased that along with us she was able to help out an old friend, and commented that our good deed for the day was done!

CHAPTER FIVE

Classy Ladies

It was yet another long Saturday night on the door in the ambrosia of life that is door work. I was working with my mate Tommy. We started at 7.30pm and had managed to turn away a steady stream of pissed up people and had chucked out a couple of stag parties very early on. It was all pretty standard as things go, with maybe the exception of the 'Super Classy' middle aged ladies dressed in burlesque outfits, with muffin tops and more cellulite than an orange grove. They were not the most attractive bunch to look at, and when they opened their mouths… my god! You've never heard the likes of it! I had to Google some of the swear words just to see what the hell they meant. They ranged in age from early twenties up to the Granny of the bride to be; with her teeth like a council fence and a straw in the shape of a cock hanging round her neck, which complimented her hairy top lip which was manlier than moustaches on some young lads these days.

When you get a big group of them like that, they can be bad enough to start with, but one of my all-time pet hates is whistles. They just come in and blow them and blow them so much it would put a time served prostitute to shame! So, call me a spoilsport, or a 'grumpy old bastard' as 'Granny Tash' called me on the way in, but I confiscated all of the whistles telling they could have them back on the way out. Half an hour later, in a packed bar, above the cackles of 'Jabba the Hutts' daughters, I could hear the shrill of a whistle over and over and over again.

As I went into the bar and started to look for the clever arse that had the whistle I got the manager in my earpiece over the radio saying "For Fucks sake, Stu, stick that whistle right up her Jacksie will you? It's doing my head in" "Oh don't you worry I bloody will", I replied and so off I went in search of the phantom whistler. Yeah you guessed it, it was old Granny tash. She had a pink referee whistle hanging out of her mouth blowing and blowing and blowing, actually she had the look of an over the hill prostitute to think of it.

So I went over, tapped her on the shoulder and said "can I take the whistle until you leave please?" she just ignored me, as I expected. So again I said the same thing. This time she smiled at me with her chess board teeth, well that would be if chess boards were black and yellow as opposed to black and white, laughed and said "what was that you wanted son, me naked body rubbed all over you?" The very thought of her wrinkled, leather skinned body mixed with the smell of her breath was almost enough to make me heave! "Beautiful as you are I'm afraid I must decline your very tempting offer" I replied, my tone sarcastic. She cackled like a witch on acid which just made the acrid smell of her breath all the worse, you could just tell by looking, or even smelling this horror, that she'd had more cock than Bernard Matthews!

"Give me the whistle now or you're leaving'", I said trying to disguise the look of complete and utter disgust on my face. "Oh you want my whistle son" she said "I don't know about that but you can have my cherry if that's any good for you son". The mouthy, stagnant old trout that she was, she then dropped the whistle down her saggy cleavage and with another acrid smelling cackle said "There you go lover get it out with your teeth".

The whistle had a long ribbon hanging from it, sticking out of the saggy tits that no doubt would hide her feet with no bra on and probably resembled an ordnance survey map, or an A to Z. So I made a grab for the ribbon, ready to pull the poor whistle out and take my own personal bit of glory to shut this old tart up. But just as a I grabbed it and pulled on the ribbon of doom, she shouted "epee you cheeky little fucker, look lasses he is trying to cop a feel", and then it happened; the most embarrassing night on the door ever, up came her knee and with all the force of a JCB combined with the skill of 50 years fighting in the bingo, she kneed me right in the bollocks.

The Diaries of a Doorman

It felt like being hit by a truck, all I could smell was her breath and all I could hear was Tommy on radio pissing himself laughing as my face turned white, and then no doubt quickly to red. The pain in the family jewels rose up into my stomach and I fell on my knees, with granny tash bloody shouting and laughing "look lasses he is going down on me now!" I was fuming at this point and I quickly recovered my composure, not too sure about my self-respect though, and made a grab for her to throw her out. That's when the kicking, screaming and flaying of arms with sharp curly talons going for my face, began.

"Right that's it!" I shouted as I bent forward, picked her up and chucked her over my shoulder in a fireman's lift. She was kicking and screaming all the way, as I began to carry her to the door to throw her out. This is where I saw Tommy, totally buckled with laughter. As I put her down on the path outside of the door she was still going off on one, trying to attack me and shouting and swearing with all of the decorum of an ally cat. The rest of her group began drifting towards the door. They all thought it was hilarious, and one woman shouted out to her, "Hope it doesn't rain, we're all staying here for more drinks, so you will just have to wait until we come out". Well as you can imagine she wasn't too happy at all with that as the rest of her group all started drifting back to the bar to order more colourful jugs of whatever the hell they were drinking.

Just then, someone must have been looking down on me and arranged my revenge of this absolute savage, as the heavens just opened. Rain poured down bouncing off the ground, absolutely soaking this sorry excuse for a lady. Well I really did try my very best not to laugh, but wasn't having much luck, as I stood just inside the shelter of the doorway as she began to resemble more and more a geriatric drowned rat. Just as quickly as it started, the rain stopped. The rest of the group started making their way back out of the bar all laughing at the sodden wet soggy mess that was waiting for them, and off they went to another bar. I really should have radioed the other bars but what would I have said? Be on the lookout for a very old woman, dressed in a pink burlesque outfit, with teeth like a council fence who ten minutes ago has just single handed dropped me in the middle of my own bar????

CHAPTER SIX

Ginger Powers

Well what can you say about this lad, Peely aka Ginger Powers. This is the man that got me back into the game again after giving it up for quite a few years, I regret massively going back into this game now as it cost me more than I would have ever thought possible, but that another story. The first time I met this huge mentalist was when he started working on the door at my local pub. Being an ex-doorman at the time I always made a point of saying hello to the lads, showing them a bit of respect and having a bit crack on like you do, I suppose in a way this was the thing I missed, the crack and the banter.

We seemed to get on straight away and the crack and banter was great. Week after week I would go out on the beer, Peely would go to work, and we would end up having a good laugh. I told him that I always had his back, to which at first I think he was a little sceptical as at 5ft 9" I am not the biggest around by far and this lad is 6ft 3, and a controlled madman to say the very least, but as it sometimes does in this game one night it came out on top, and I managed to help out, but the less said about this scenario the better! This night ended up being a great night with a couple of my mates, and a couple of Peely's mates that later became good friends of mine.

This included the oddly named 'Dolly' who's party trick was to go to the bar and politely ask for an empty glass when he was pissed, puke in it and then put it back on the bar and say 'thank you' (Dirty bastard, makes me cockle every time). Along with Millar who at the time was the only MOT inspector that I had ever met who had a driving ban for drink driving.

Anyway one of my mates, who we shall leave unnamed I think, told us that his cousin was having a party so we all decided to go. When we got out of the taxi, we were on a quiet street. My mate seemed a little confused as to which house it was. Eventually he picked one. It was a large, nice looking, 1920's semi and he started banging on the door. While it was obvious to me that there was no-one home, no lights on, nobody answering the door, he was adamant that this was where his cousin lived and had invited us all to party.

After ten minutes of banging on the door he scratched his head and said "Arrrr Fuck It" and proceeded to kick the front door in insisting that his cousin wouldn't mind. Well I couldn't help but fall about laughing. So in we went, me, Peely, Dolly, Millar, the lad that kicked the door in and another mate of mine called Mark. Once we were inside we hit the fridge which was full of bottles of Becks and Bud, but no-one had a bottle opener. I nearly lost a tooth trying to pop mine open with my teeth and then out pops Dolly with his now trade mark bottle opener. This was about 6 or 7 years ago, and by coincidence I saw Dolly just last night, and he still had the very same bottle opener.

Anyway, the party started to get into full swing, the doors were wide open, the music was blasting and then the lad who kicked the door in got a phone call from his cousin. The same cousin who owned the house that we were in, or did he? "Where are you?" He said "Told you we are partying, where's Stu and Peely?" his cousin replied. "I am at your house like I said, oh and by the way, you were late so I kicked your door in" said my mate.

All we heard at this point was laughter down the phone. Louder and louder. It was the sort of laugh that couldn't help but make you start laughing along with him, a bit like the old laughing policeman. That's when he said down the phone "Are you in my house in North Shields?" "Well yeah where else would I be?" replied my mate. The laughter started again and the cousin then reminded him that he had moved to a new house in Tynemouth some six months previous. Well as you can imagine, my mate just went white and we all just fell about laughing. We rang a taxi, and as the taxi pulled up so did the police. We explained the situation and, give him his due, my mate took all the blame, admitted what had happened and paid for the damage to the front door. He also replaced the contents of the fridge.

This is when I decided to go back on the door. The last licence I had was the old council licence, so I had to go to a door supervisor training course in order to qualify to be able to apply for an SIA licence to be able to legally work on the door again. I have got to say some of the best times of my 'door life' were working with this big ginger nutcase, some nights I went home exhausted from laughing at his stories.

Not just a laugh, Peely is a seriously hard bloke. What I like about him is that he is fair, never one to raise a fist in anger, and would only lash out and hit someone when he had no other choice. Now in the pub that we worked in, there was quite a lot of trouble and it was filled with some very handy people, you know there's always a pub like that I any town.

During the time I was there, it was like World War 3 on many occasions. It was one of those places that when one person kicked off, all the other punters seemed to be related to each other in some way, so they would all kick off. Many a time we had to more or less fight for our lives in that place, which was when working with this bloke came in handy. In all of the episodes that we have had over the years, and all of the times that we have had to fight off some very very naughty people; every punch I have ever seen Peely throw has without fail, been a knockout. One punch and off to sleep. It became a running joke that if there was a kick off and it got too bad that we had no option that to fight for our own safety that I should have just stood behind the aggressor with my arms out ready to catch them when Peely out them to sleep, lower them to the ground and get them in the recovery position. This bloke has ended up being one of the best friends that I have ever had. If I ever need anything, no matter what, all I have to do is pick up the phone and vice versa, I am sure he will agree. It's a shame that he retired from the door. I miss working with him and I can honestly say he is the best I have ever worked with.

In the spring of 2013 he rang me with some bad news, very bad news. An altercation had taken place in his local pub over the Christmas period, which ended up with the manager having a smashed cheek bone and a broken shoulder, and Peely at crown court facing five years. I didn't know the full story at the time, but I knew that something wasn't right. He is not one to just lash out for no reason. I arranged that I would pick him up and take him to court on the day. He had pleaded guilty to section 18 wounding, but with extenuating circumstances.

I went over to his house for a cuppa to see him before the court date and got the full story. Between Christmas and New Year Peely and his partner of many years, and mother to his beautiful baby Sienna, had been drinking in a local bar, a bar in which I had drank with them on many an occasion before. They stayed late for a 'Private Party' shall we say. The manager of the pub, supposedly a friend of Peely and Emma's had been, for want of a better word, 'touchy feely' with Emma a few times over the night and Peely had told him to behave. He had also been making lurid comments to Emma when Peely couldn't hear. Emma didn't tell him as she didn't want any trouble.

Later in the night Peely went off to the gents and when he came back Emma had no choice but to tell him what was going on as it has begun to get worse. As soon as Peely had gone to the gents the pervy manager had moved his chair from the other side of the bar next to Emma, he kept trying to touch her leg and was making perverted comments. When Peely came back from the Gents, Emma went over to him and said she wanted to go home, she was visibly upset and told him what was going on.

Peely walked over to the pub manager and pushed him in the side of the face with an open palm, as a warning if you like. A combination of Peely's strength and the managers intoxication, caused the manager to fall backwards from the stool and hit his face, and shoulder, on the corner of the pool table. This knocked him unconscious. The manager, even though it was clear to see on CCTV, told a cock and bull story and it ended up in court. I will never forget going to pick him up for court and him saying goodbye to his youngest baby daughter. I had tears in my eyes, he will deny it but I know he did as well. We walked to the car in silence, carrying with us his black leather sports bag that was in effect his 'prison bag', and got into my car.

Parking the car seemed to be the easy bit, the walk from the car to the court was like walking 'the green mile', I carried the 'prison bag' and typically I carried it through security, where they found razors in the bag and confiscated them. These were shaving razors just before you think anything bad. Once at court it seemed to take ages to find the right court room, as each time we got to the correct room, they changed it. This happened 3, or maybe 4, times. Eventually we found the room and went in. Peely was locked in the dock with security guards behind him. Myself, Emma and Kayleigh all sat in the public gallery. All the worry, all that preparation, not only for him but for his family was wasted as the judge adjourned the case almost immediately. The chief prosecution witness, the pervy manager, didn't bother to show up.

Two months later we returned. It seemed like yesterday that we had last walked 'the green mile' to court. This time I made him carry his own bag through security! Once we were in the court, surprise surprise, we found out that the chief prosecution witness / pervy pub manager hadn't shown up again! This time the judge was annoyed, and rightly so. This bloke was costing the tax payer a fortune by making wild allegations, bringing a court case at crown court and not even turning up. The judge adjourned the case again, but this time for two hours, in which he instructed to clerk of the courts to summon the police who would be instructed to find the witness and bring him to court.

Time seemed to stand still. I waited and watched the clock ticking but it never seemed to go any faster. We went to the canteen for a coffee and then went for a walk outside before returning to the court.

The Diaries of a Doorman

I was 100% sure that the police would not manage to get this wanker to court. He had obviously made things up and didn't want to give his account on oath in court. About 2 and half hours from the adjournment, the court usher came through the doors and shouted for Mr Peel. This was it! I watched Peely hug and kiss his Son Rhys, Daughter Kayleigh and his partner Emma. He then turned to me and said "I know who my friends are Stu, look after them". He more or less picked me up and hugged me, I was ready for tears myself by this time.

As we walked into the court again, Peely was led to the dock and locked in with guards. To my complete and utter shock I saw sitting in the witness box the star witness, the dirty old perv that had caused this in the first place. I think we were all in shock, he sat there, the little rat, with his head down in the witness box, unable to look anyone in the eye. I thought this was going to end up being a terrible day. Poor Rhys was meant to be celebrating his 16th Birthday that day. I felt for him. The case began and Emma gave her evidence first, which the prosecution tried, but didn't manage, to discredit her. How can you discredit someone who is telling the truth?

Next up was the super witness himself. The Judge informed him that there was CCTV of the whole incident which he would play, and he asked the witness to talk him through what had happened on the night. The next part did surprise me, and it just shows how absolutely thick and stupid someone can be. There were two large screen monitors in front of him, playing CCTV of the night in question and the incident. You could have heard a pin drop when he was giving his evidence.

He had his head down, he didn't seem to be able to look at the judge, or the prosecution barrister, never mind any of the defence. So he began by telling his tall tale of what happened that night. The court clerk was running through the CCTV footage, pausing and asking the witness what his recollection of the night was. His story was completely different to the CCTV version that was there for all to see. I couldn't believe it. The CCTV backed up the evidence given by both Peely and Emma. The Judge looked really pissed off. This idiot was standing up in Crown Court, telling blatant lies.

Stu Armstrong

The Judge summed up and said that a custodial sentence of 5 years could passed which worried us, but he passed sentence of 300 hours community service and one year probation due to the level of injuries that 'Mr liar liar pants on fire' sustained and the fact that he still, some six months later, had still not regained the feeling in the right side of his face.

He also ruled that Peely threw a punch rather than a push, and to round it off rather nicely, he also ruled that the manager was not allowed to claim for criminal injuries. As the judge was summing up, Peely got up and started to walk out of the court, to which the judge reminded him that he was still talking. It was funny to see him go a few shades or red, his cheeks also matched his hair! When we came out of the court it was a beautiful sunny day. I went to fetch my car from a nearby car park and couldn't resist putting the roof down and pumping up the tunes. I picked them up from the front of the court building. We had a quick blast back to his house with Emma and Kayleigh's hair attacking him in the wind!

Pleased that a custodial sentence wasn't passed down it's still a pretty high price to pay to defend your partner from a lecherous, perverted, lying bastard!!!!!

CHAPTER SEVEN

Life Savers

Doormen are seen by many people, and portrayed in the media, as violent nasty thugs and an all-round pack of complete and utter bastards, this is not true. There is another side of the job that people often don't see as it is never splashed all over the news or social media. These are the times when we go out of our way and put ourselves in serious danger to help someone and, in many occasions, save someone's life.

Over the years I have been instrumental in helping people in different situations. I have actually saved people lives on more than one occasion. From the woman who had a fit, knocked herself unconscious and started to choke on her own tongue, to the bloke that passed out in the middle of a nightclub and was literally dying in the middle of the dance floor not breathing, no pulse nothing. But there's one notable story that shows that even when you do good things and potentially lay your own life on the line, it can come back to haunt you.

At the end of a busy Saturday night a number of years ago we got to the best time of the night, closing time. I walked around the bar shouting "Come on folks, see your drinks off and make your way outside!" I could feel the tiredness creeping over me, it had been a bloody long night. The bar had been packed, we had no trouble to speak of, but it had just dragged and dragged. As the last people filtered slowly out of the door, I wished them goodnight and off they went into the darkness.

The other doorman was doing the toilet checks, just to make sure that nobody was asleep in there, or hiding and I sat down just as the pub manager brought us a couple of pints over. Sitting having a quiet pint at the end of the shift is a great way to wind down and it's great crack chatting shit with the other doormen. We were having bit of a laugh. You really do need to wind down after a shift when you do this sort of work, it's impossible to go straight home and straight to bed, and if you do, you're lying awake half the night!

As we were sitting chatting I heard a scream. A very loud scream, and then again and again and again. The ear splitting shriek was coming from outside the back of the pub and it sounded like a woman. We put our pints down and ran out of the back door and around the corner to where the screams were coming from. We saw a staggering man, his face covered in blood and a woman being attacked by a big gang of lads. They were really laying into her, punching her hard over and over again and laughing. One lad was giving her very hard punches to the stomach, kidneys and chest.

There were around ten or so lads. I would guess that they were ranging in age from around 18 to 20 years old. The man and the woman who were being attacked were in their early 20's. They were a married couple that had in fact been in my bar earlier that night. As we ran up towards them, they let go of her and started to square up to us. As they let go of her legs just seemed to buckle and she dropped to the floor still screaming, I think in shock.

As myself and Tommy got closer, about half of the lads ran away. However, one of them started kicking the already bloodied husband, who was still on the floor, and another stated kicking the woman. We got closer and were shouting, I don't even know what, it was all so quick. Tommy ran into two of them, like some kind of machine. They didn't stand a chance. Tommy grabbed one under each arm and ran them into the shutters of a closed shop dropping them both in a heap.

That left the other three of the group with me running full tilt at them, trying to use the forward momentum, I ran directly into one of them with my hands open palmed out in front of me at chest height. I shoved one of them half way across the road and down onto his arse. At this point I am pretty sure one ran away, but I can't be certain, I only remember dealing with the other one by cracking a right hook to his chin that sent him crashing to the pavement.

The Diaries of a Doorman

The husband with the bloodied face dragged himself up off the ground and over towards his wife. Myself and Tommy gently picked up the woman with one of her arms around my neck, and the other around Tommy's. Just then, blue lights started flashing and a police car came screeching to a halt just next to us, it seemed that the manager of the pub, and a local kebab shop owner had both called the police.

It seemed odd to me as there were three police officers in the car, two men and a woman. It was strange because the police always seem to be either alone, or there are two of them, don't suppose it really matters, but I can't ever remember seeing three together. Anyway the lads who had caused all of this were still hanging around and the two young policemen went over to try and talk to them while the police woman came with me and Tommy as we carried the woman, followed by her husband, into my pub to sit her down. For every step we made the woman let out a wince of pain and I was a little worried about her breathing, she seemed to be taking very short, sharp intakes of air.

Once inside we managed to sit her down. The pub manager comes over with glasses of water for the husband and wife, and then locked the back door. The policewoman took one look at the women and radioed in for an Ambulance. She started asking what had happened, it turned out that it had started as an argument over a Kebab!

Just then something came over the policewoman's earpiece and she ran to the door shouting "let me out quick open the door, open the door!" With a shocked look on his face, the bar manager unlocked the door and she ran out, followed by me and Tommy to see the two young policemen massively outnumbered, being attacked by what had now grown in size to a group of about twenty. Without thinking both me and Tommy ran into the melee and got stuck in. We were lashing out 'Geordie Windmill' style and luckily seconds later three police cars, closely followed by a couple of police vans, came flying round the corner. Most of the lads ran off, some of them got caught and some were cuffed and dragged into the van.

A few minutes later the ambulance arrived and took both the man and woman away. We went back into the pub and made sure everything was locked up. Our adrenaline was still pumping as we went to finish our pints, which we then found out were gone as the manager had decided to chuck them down the sink while we were playing at World War three out the back. Nice of him! Six months later I was standing on the door of the same bar about 9pm on a Saturday night when this woman came up to me and said that I was her hero. I had no idea who she was and probably said something like "Yeah Pet, I am everybody's hero me". She asked if she could buy me a drink for after my shift and I still had no idea who she was, but hey don't look a gift horse in the mouth!

She came back from the bar a while later with a bloke and told us there were two pints behind the bar for us we finished. The bloke that she was in with I recognised at the time, but wasn't sure where from. All of a sudden, like a bolt from the blue, I remembered who he was, He was the 'Kebab attack Husband' as we had started referring to him. So that must be 'Donna' as we referred to her, as in, Donner Kebab!!!

We got talking and they were full of thanks. I found out that she had actually ended up with a punctured lung, that explained the breathing that night. According to her she would have been dead if not for us saving her. It was nice catching up with them again and good to see that they were both ok, but the gratitude bit was getting a little embarrassing. As time went on I would see more and more of them in the bar and we sort of became friends the three of us. We got on pretty well when they were in the bar.

One Saturday night a few months later, just as we were emptying the bar, the manager shouted, "Stu, there's a phone call in the back for you". This worried me straight away as I never got calls to the bar. I was sure something was wrong, everything was going through my mind. Could it be the kids? I shouted back "coming mate, who is it?" "Not sure, just some bird" the manager said "Said you would know who she was". As I went to the office, I didn't have a clue who was on the other end of the phone "Hello?" The voice came crying down the receiver at me "Is that Stu? Stu you got to help me, my husband has just had a heart attack and is in hospital, I just don't know what to do and I knew that you would". Shocked at what she had said I realised it was 'Donna'. I was confused, why had she rung me? What the hell could I do? I took her number, told her I would ring her back and put the phone down. What the hell could I do? I crumpled up the piece of paper with her number on and threw it in the bin.

By then I was working with a different lad on the door, my best mate at the time. I told him all about it and he thought that I was as odd as I thought. That night we had arranged to meet some of the lads, all off duty bouncers, in one of the local nightclubs for a beer and a bit crack on. One beer for me as I was always the driver. We got down to the club and bypassed the queue. We shook hands with the lads on the door and managed to get in without paying, one of the perks of being a doorman. We met the lads and were having a laugh talking about things that had happened to us all that night. I told the lads about my call and they all cracked up laughing when one the lads said " Well Stu mate, isn't there some kind of old Chinese proverb that says if you save someone's life then you have to lookout for them for ever, or fucking something like that?" We all fell about laughing.

I am not sure why, but that phone call played on my mind for the rest of the night. I still don't know what I could have done. I left the club about 3.30am and I drove to the hospital, stopped out front and looked into the accident and emergency department. I could see this woman pacing backwards and forwards up the waiting room in tears.

I parked up, got out, and went inside. When she saw me she came running over sobbing, and throwing her arms around me. She was saying over and over again "I knew you would come Stu, I just knew you would come!" "Well you knew more than I did then" I said "I am not sure exactly what I am supposed to do, would you not be better off ringing some family to come and sit with you". But no, apparently I was the only one that knew what to do. Well I didn't have a clue. Through the tears she said "Will you come to intensive care with me as they won't tell me anything?" Why not what harm will it do?' I thought and off we went through the deserted corridors of the hospital. All you could hear was the echo of her tears reverberating around the empty corridors.

When we eventually got to Intensive care, she asked how he was and all she was being told was that as well as expected, which I think wasn't really of any help to her. She just sat down and started sobbing again. I went over to the desk and said "Look, I am friend of the family, this woman is sitting there not knowing of her husband is going to die or live and all you can say is he is as well as can be expected, not really very helpful is it? How would you like to be in her shoes?" The nurse in charge saw my point and went over to her to have a chat. She explained that the prognosis was good for a full recovery, but the next 8 to 12 hours would be critical, and that she couldn't see him until morning. The nurse told her to go home for some rest. She eventually agreed to go home to change and get some of her husband's things before returning.

"Look, I have the car outside, I will drop you off on my way home at your house for you to get sorted" I said. With muffled thanks she tried to cling onto me, her arms tight around me. I give her a friendly hug and get her into the car. When we got to her house she asked me to come in, I said no. I was shattered by this time and just wanted to go home to bed. She moaned on and on and on and I suppose it wore me down. As soon as I stepped through the door I got a feeling that something wasn't right, that she had lured me into her house with ulterior motives. I thought 'no don't be so stupid that would just be callous', but I started making excuses, I wanted out of there, and quick. Excuses made, she ran upstairs shouting "I am just going to get changed, come up and then will you drop me back at the hospital?" 'Hmmm maybe I was right". I shouted up the stairs "Listen I will drop you at the hospital, but I will wait outside in the car and have a tab" and I got out of there and into the safety of the car!

A few minutes later she came out and I dropped her back at the hospital. Then off I went home to bed, into a long lovely slumber that took me until about lunch time the following day. The following week, again on the door at the same bar, she came in and thanked me for the previous weekend. She explained that her husband was out of hospital and doing well. I told her how pleased I was, it was awkward, I didn't want anything to do with her in that respect but I just was getting the feeling that she wanted more and she just didn't leave me alone. Over the following months she would came into the pub again and again and again and each time she would run up to me and hug me, she seemed to be becoming more and more flirtatious towards me. I still wasn't interested in the slightest, and I started to feel sorry for her husband, maybe I got it wrong , maybe she was just friendly but it was getting right on my titts! It was like having my very own stalker and I actually dreaded going to work, this went on for a good while, months and months in fact until I was ready to tell her to go and fill her pockets with stones and take a long walk of a short pier, and then all of a sudden it just seemed to have stopped, disappeared, vanished, gone. Well I was pretty chuffed about that as I am sure that you can imagine, since then I have moved bars so hopefully she will never find me. So I guess there is only a few explanations here, either I got it wrong or her husband topped her!

CHAPTER EIGHT

THE HORSE SHOE BAR

The run up to Christmas 1995 was a very odd, but a very lucrative one for me, thanks to a job that I was asked to do for a large well known brewery. It has to be, to this day, the oddest job that I have ever done. The brewery was a large one at the time, with hundreds of managed houses. I was doing quite a bit of work for them at the time all, over the North East of England. All of the jobs were pretty unremarkable, until this one. At stupid o-clock in the morning, off in the distance I heard the shriek of the phone ringing, each ring feeling like an axe running through my hung-over head. I climbed from my bed and stumbled to the phone, answering it with a grunt, only to hear the all too cheery voice of the brewery area manager.

Quickly coming to my senses, I listened as he described a job that he wanted me to do. The more he explained, the weirder it sounded. He wanted me to be in Hartlepool that day by 5pm, in a bar called the Powlett. I thought about it, I didn't think that I had ever thought about Hartlepool before, let alone set foot in the town that is famous for hanging a monkey! But this wasn't just the normal run of the mill door job; he wanted me on site 24 hours a day 7 days a week. The caveat to this job was that I wasn't allowed to leave the premises, not for anything with the exception of a fire, flood or bomb I was told. Thinking about it in hindsight, maybe I was mad, but I was thinking of a doorman's rate for 24 hours a day, 7 days a week and even back then that came to a lot of money. Not that doorman's pay has ever bloody kept up with the rate of inflation!

Thinking about it, £10 an hour, 24 hours a day... as I did the calculations in my head, I was like a cartoon cat with pound signs in my eyes kerchinnnnng! That was £1680 a week, not to be sniveled at. But why did they want me there 24 hours a day 7 days a week? The thought of the cash, a few weeks in the run up to Christmas, was just too good to ignore; especially since at the time I was driving an old Fiesta XR2 that had seen better days.

Each time I thought about the job, I thought about the money and I thought about a new car. So after mulling it over for all of ten minutes, I thought fuck it, don't look a gift horse in the mouth. I packed a bag with the essentials that I thought I would need, checked in the XR2 and off I went down to the bizarre mythological land that lies south of the river Tyne! I had no clue where the bar was, I don't think that I had ever in my life been to Hartlepool but knew it was off the A19, about 20 miles or so south of the Tyne Tunnel. I was flying down the A19 blasting some Christmas tunes out of the stereo. I was quite pleased with myself and wasn't really worrying what was in store for me.

As soon as I saw the sign for the slip road off the A19 signposted for Hartlepool, off I went to the land that time forgot! It really was like stepping back in time driving through the part of Hartlepool that I was in, I still don't know to this day what area of Hartlepool this was but it was a stinking, shit-pit of a place. I remember thinking to myself that it even made the infamous Meadowell in North Shields look posh!

(It should be noted that some years later, in fact more than a decade later I drove through the same part of Hartlepool and hardily recognised the place, it's amazing what you can do with a bulldozer and some government grants.)

So after going back on myself and getting myself lost a few times, I asked for directions in a garage. I finally found the bar. It was a huge pub set on a roundabout in the shape of a horse shoe. When I pulled into the car park it didn't look at all bad, so I parked the car up and to walked into the pub. The doors were locked. I went to the other entrance that seemed to take you into a smaller back bar, and this was also locked. I noticed that the glass upper section of the door was smashed and boarded over. The more I looked around, the more boarded over windows I saw; alarm bells were ringing in my ears, why wasn't the pub open? Why were around a third of the windows smashed? And last but not least, was there a burnt out Ford Orion on the corner of the car park?

I told myself that I was already there, there was a lot of money to be made here and I had my heart set on a new car. So I started banging as loud as I could on the door for what seemed like an eternity, in the bitter cold. In my entire life I have never known it not be cold and windy in Hartlepool, but maybe that's just me. I was still banging and banging on the door, I could hear dogs barking, but nothing else.

As I stood it started to snow, not enough to turn the drab black tarmac car park white, but enough to make you shiver when combined with the ice cold wind that came from the North Sea. I waited for about half an hour, I was used to this area manager being late. I then went back to the car and dug out my mobile phone. Mobile maybe not being the right word for it, it was like a bloody brick. I turned it on end, pulled out the extending aerial and dialed Mike, the area manager. He answered quite quickly, the line was bad, the line was always bad on this phone, "Mike" I said, "Its Stu, I am sat outside this bar in Hartlepool like a bloody half-baked arse hole, its freezing cold, the pub is shut and no-one will answer, I can hear some dogs barking but that's it, not even a light on".

The silence on the line was deafening, and long, "Mike, you there mate?" I asked and still there was silence. Then came the outburst that I had a feeling was going to blurt from Mike's mouth. Mike, a tall prematurely grey, hoarded man in his early 40's, had worked his way up from being a barman in some pub managed by the same brewery somewhere in the west end of Newcastle. He wasn't exactly known for his 'Management Speak' shall we say. "You fucking what? The pubs not open? You sure Stu?" with sarcasm heavy in my voice I replied, "Err no Mike I am not sure, I am sitting inside in the warm having a bastard pint! What do you think, of course it's sodding well shut or I wouldn't have rang and said it wasn't open now would I?" Again came the deafening silence on the other end of the line and he said "Stu, hang on five minutes and I will ring you back" and down went the phone, no thank you, kiss your arse or anything.

'Here we go' I thought to myself. I liked Mike but none of the jobs he put my way were ever straight forward. I had heard a rumor that he had told more than one person that he passed on his 'Poison Chalice jobs to me, I was starting to wonder if maybe this was true. So, true to form half an hour later my oversized mobile phone warbles its fucked up tune at me, and I answered to hear Mikes voice verbally vomiting down the phone at me with the force of a cyclone on acid! "The stupid fucking cowardly piece of shit bastard Stu, that's what he is, what in the fuck am I going to do now?" Telling me that, this bloke has royally pissed on me from a great height, the wanker opened the bar this morning and shut it two hours later and fucked off, can you believe this complete bell-end?" "Errr calm down Mike will you, I don't have the first idea what you're talking about here" I said, as he ranted on, telling me the sorry story of why the pub wasn't open. It seemed to get windier and windier, an icy cold wind blowing on from the North Sea trying it's very best to pick up my little XR2 and blow it away.

For a few months they had been having a lot of trouble in the bar, I learned from Mike as he started to calm down. Robberies, break-in's, fights, drugs, you name it. He also told me that the manager and his family had called him up recently and said they had had enough, and were moving out that day. He also told me that he was having great problems in getting a relief manager to go into the Powlett and to re-open it; seemingly it had gained somewhat of a reputation as a trouble bar over the last few months.

Mike told me that he was coming down with a set of keys, and on the way he arranged for a relief manager to come and open the bar. I knew then why it was a 24 hour, 7 day a week job. I was a doorman when the bar was open, and live in security when it wasn't. Oh Well, I thought to myself, what the hell, It can't be all that bad. Just as I had expected, half an hour came and went and there was no Mike. This blokes timekeeping was unreal, and by unreal I mean fucking terrible! I must have drifted off into a deep sleep in the car; I still had a blinding hangover from the night before. The next thing I felt was my whole car rocking and an incessant banging noise.

I awoke quickly with a start to find Mike banging on my windscreen and some other bloke rocking my car backwards from side to side, both sniggering.

I suppose it was the best to say to my area manager, but I didn't know where the hell I was "Fuck off you bastards, FUCK OFFFFFFFFF!" I screamed, still not 100% sure of who it was, or even where I was for that matter. I jumped out of the car giving the knob-head that was shaking my car a push to the chest, maybe a little too hard, as he flew back and over an old concrete planter falling flat on his arse. Well it served him right. Mike thought this was hilarious, rolling with laughter, he said between breaths "Some Bouncer you are Stu, you nearly shit yourself there." Anyway, into the pub we went. We switched the lights on and it seemed like a decent bar inside, not massively modern, but not really old and stinking either. I was introduced to the bloke that I had just dropped in the car park, he was called Dave. Dave was a relief manager from the brewery that was going to, with my help apparently, open the bar again.

So we get sorted, and most importantly I got Mike to agree and sign a timesheet for me starting at the time that I had arrived on site, long before my little granddad nap in the car. When I asked about not going off site, I was told that I could order takeaways for food and the company would pay for them. After all the preliminary work off went Mike, sniggering and calling over his shoulder, "good luck lads!" I couldn't help thinking that I was being stitched up, but I put that thought to the back of my mind and had a swift pint while Dave was preparing to open up. I took my stuff upstairs to the flat above the pub, which was completely empty of all furniture; in fact the only thing that did litter the rooms was a couple of random dog turds, in every room but one. Dave hadn't been upstairs yet, so you can guess which room I set up home in cant you!

That got me thinking about the stinking Stone Henge type monuments of shit all over the house combined with the barking that I could hear earlier. Just as the thought entered my head I heard a whine, a long high pitched whine like a dog crying, which seemed to come from a window. It was dark outside, so I couldn't see out, but I managed to find a torch. I opened the window to climb out and take a look, when I shone the torch I could see a big flat roof, again covered in monuments of dog shit. As I slid the window fully open I started to slide my legs out onto the dark shit sodden flat roof when all of a sudden I heard the barking and growling again, but this time it was a lot closer.

I could see two dark shapes at the other side of the roof; this was where the noise was coming from. The breath of the dark figures heavy in the cold night air, "these must be the shit machines" I remember thinking to myself. Just a split second later all hell was let loose as the two 'hounds of the bloody Baskervilles' let rip, running across the roof snarling and growling, heading straight for me and my legs which were outside the window on the roof. I scrambled back inside with a split second to spare before the teeth of two huge German shepherds turned by legs into doggy treats.

The window slammed. I looked out and immediately felt sorry for the two beast like creatures out in the cold. They looked half starved. I snuck down into the dry stockroom without Dave seeing and grabbed a full card of bags of pork scratching's, and went back upstairs. Looking out of the window I couldn't see the dogs at first and then realized that they were off in the far corner of the roof where there seemed to be some shelter from the biting wind. It took what seemed like forever to open all the bags of scratching's, but at last they were open. Slowly and quietly I opened the window and chucked out the mountain of hairy pork snatchings onto the roof and put down a huge bowl of water. I shouted and sure enough like the dispels of the devil these two big smelly beasts ran towards me again, this time I was ready and closed to window tight before they got there. When they sniffed out the meaty treats left for them, they devoured them within seconds and furiously lapped the water.

I found out later that night, from a regular punter in the bar, that the dogs had belonged to the manager and they had left them there the week before when they left the pub and buggered off to Spain. I don't know how they could do that, it disgusted me. I ended up having them collected the next afternoon by the RSPCA, and by then they were no more ferocious than pink fluffy bunnies. But the stocks of crisps and porky scratching's were gone and the bellies of the dogs were full, I guess they were just starving.

Dave, who had still not been upstairs, gave me a shout and told me he was about ready to open up. I went down with a uniform of sorts on, black trousers, black leather gloves, black coat and a black hat. All I needed was a black mask and a bag marked 'Swag' and you could have mistaken me for a burglar! As I swung open the main doors of the pub I was surprised to see a woman standing there in the shadows, no more than 25 years old and with a figure to die for. I couldn't quite see her face in the darkness as she blurted out, "Mind I want paid for all day, not my fucking fault the bar didn't get opened is it?" Such a venomous voice came from the girl with the amazing figure. She turned out to be Sharon the barmaid, and as she walked in, out of the doom and gloom, I was expecting some great beauty to appear before me, but in reality as soon as I saw her face I started to laugh, she was no looker to say the last, this lass was full on fugly! (Fugly = Fucking Ugly). To top it off, she had an attitude to match, although I am sure her heart was in the right place, at least I hope that it was because her bloody nose wasn't!!

So the pub was open, I was on the door and it was bloody freezing. I kept thinking 'God only knows what's going to happen here, must be bad if the last relief manager just buggered off'. The punters started coming in, a good mix, a lot of older people who I took to be the regulars in the bar and a hoard of younger ones in the lounge, some of them very young indeed. In fact they were so young I wouldn't even let them in. When I was asking for ID most of them said words to the effect of "when did we ever need ID in here?" to which I replied "from now you do". After about half an hour the bar was pretty full, the street outside and the car park all looked quiet; so I went inside for a walk around.

I saw a very shifty bloke watching my every move, knowing something wasn't right I ignored him and when I saw that all was ok inside I went back on the door. I positioned myself so that I could see the shifty looking bloke through the window. Soon enough two lads went over to him had a bit crack on, and then all three of them

The Diaries of a Doorman

went to the gents. In I went after them and found the two other lads handing over shifty money, obviously a dealer I thought as I grabbed him by the scruff of the neck and dragged him out through the bar, at the same time I shouted to the now busy lounge "we don't have drugs in this bar!"

I got him to the door somewhat roughly and shoved him outside. "That's it, you're barred!", I shouted. "I am not having people selling gear in here" to which he replied "big mistake you have no idea who the fuck I am, I'll be back". Well as any doorman will tell you, we hear this time and time again and it's very rare that they do come back. I replied "What did you say there?" He snorted back at me, words like venom "Have you any idea of just who I am?" Out came my old reply, stored away in the brain, used on many such occasions as this "Well mate if you don't know who you are then how the fuck am I supposed to?" And with this he made his fingers into the shape of a gun and made a shooting motion at my head. It wasn't the first time someone had done that to me and it wasn't to be the last. He sloped off into the darkness. Funnily enough I never did see him ever again!

So that night carried on. I knocked back a couple of lads that the barmaid told me were barred, and an old man in his 70's for drinking too much of his favorite 'Amber Ale' and hitting another old bloke with his walking stick. A couple of young lads had to be ejected for dancing on the pool table with their trousers around there ankles, so all in all, when everyone was gone and I had checked the toilets and locked the doors, it seemed like it hadn't been a bad night at all.

One thing I then remembered was Mike telling me to pull all of the fruit machines into the middle of the bar away from the windows, or the windows would be smashed and the machines pulled out! So as Dave was in the cellar sorting the banking for the safe, me and the fugly barmaid had a swift pint at the bar. When we had finished I opened the door to let her out, when I heard a scream, a very loud scream filled with abject terror. It was coming from the cellar, so I picked up a pool cue and holding it like a weapon I ran downstairs to see Dave. He was white as a sheet and shaking.

"Dave, what the hell's going on who screamed?" I asked. Dave was still white as a sheet and was visibly trembling, in fact shaking like a leaf. I just couldn't get any sense out of him. So after checking the cellar to make sure there was nobody there, I took Dave upstairs, sat him down and got him a couple of large shots of whiskey. He downed them in one and started to compose himself, and slowly started to talk. He explained that he was down in the cellar and had just opened the safe, it was cold down there to start with and then he felt an icy hand on his neck, he jumped up grabbing a bottle and swung it behind him thinking he was being robbed, and saw an old man standing there. He told me that he swung the bottle with all of his force to hit the old bloke, still thinking that he was being robbed but it went straight through him, sending Dave crashing to the floor.

This sounded like bit of a tall tale to me. He carried on and said that the man laughed and then floated off up the stairs, feet not touching the ground. At first I didn't believe him, but he was so visibly shaken that I was starting to think that he must have seen something. Just then the barmaid came through giving us a shock as we had both forgotten that she was even there. She laughed and said "Oh that's only Old Jimmy, nothing to worry about!" "Old Jimmy?" I asked. She replied "Yeah old Jimmy he was the manager here in the 50's and 60's and he hung himself in the cellar, its fine we see him all the time"

I started to laugh, and Dave started to shake again. I went to the door and let the barmaid out, said goodnight and locked the doors. When I came back in Dave wasn't there, I just presumed he had went upstairs to bed, so I sat down back at the bar and slowly slipped another pint, reflecting on the day. After about five minutes Dave appeared at the bar with his bags and said "Stu, can you let me out please I can't stay here". I couldn't help but start to laugh again. "Come on Dave you big soft shite, I don't know what you saw but it wasn't Old Jimmy or whatever she said he's called, she is winding you up".

All Dave said was "for fucks sake Stu, open the fucking door I am getting out of here". I opened the door and he scuttled off to his car. With the screech of tyres and a slight smell of burning rubber, heavy in the cold night air, that was the last that I ever saw of Dave. I went upstairs, called a local takeaway and ordered some Chinese food to be delivered. Half an hour or so later it came, I checked all was locked up then settled down on the floor in the only dog shit free room, in my sleeping bag and started to eat my Chinese.

The one thing that will always stick in my mind about that night is what happened next, and no it wasn't a ghost, it wasn't a break in, it was a noodle! As I ate the noodles in the chicken chow mein I started to choke, and felt something stuck in my mouth. I put my hand in my mouth and grabbed the end of a long black hair. I pulled the hair to get it out of my mouth and started to cockle, it went right down my throat, the more I pulled, the more I coughed and choked and eventually it came out. It was matted around some noodles that I had swallowed. It was disgusting, the most horrible feeling actually pulling food up out of my throat, just the thought of it made me wretch and eventually I vomited up what was left in my stomach of the food. Obviously the Chinese lady that had cooked my meal didn't understand the concept of hair nets.

What a day it had been, but still thinking of the new car I was going to buy from this job, I settled off to sleep. I decided I would ring Mike first thing in the morning to make sure that Dave had rang him and tell him that he had dropped his arse and fucked off. After a very uncomfortable night in the sleeping bag on the floor, I woke up to the glorious bright stream of sunshine in my eyes from the curtain-less window. It was crisp and dry and bloody freezing. So I got up, got dressed, went downstairs and behind the bar and helped myself to a bottle of fresh orange and rang Mike. I think I woke him up as he sounded groggy, even though he claimed to have been up and out running already. Running my arse!

He then went ape shit for the want of a better word. Mike didn't ring him and he had no idea of the previous night's spooky entertainment. When I explained he wasn't exactly shocked when I mentioned 'Old Jimmy'. I had the feeling I was being stitched up again. He then told me that he had no other relief managers at all that could take the pub; well not until Christmas Eve anyway.

I suppose I knew what was coming next, "Stu, you were brought up in pubs weren't you? Would you run it for me for the next three weeks until the morning of Christmas eve? Please?" , "Why should I Mike?" I said "I am getting paid anyway to be on the door and as security, Its loads more extra work" to which he then replied "What if I pay you the relief managers wage on top of your door wage?" BINGO!' I thought once more with pound signs in my eyes. I found myself agreeing to a stupid idea. So I did run the pub for the next three weeks, we didn't have any major trouble, nothing out of the ordinary, and Old Jimmy didn't bother me. However I did keep seeing a figure out of the corner of my eye when the pub was shut, sitting at a table. Always the same table, but when I looked properly there was nobody there, and often in the mornings when I came down there was an empty pint glass on the table. Not a clean one but dirty one, with tiny dregs of Best Scotch in it.

The morning of Christmas Eve came and I got an early phone called from Mike at the Brewery, "Stu, you have done a great job in the pub" he said. "Do you want it permanently as the manager?" I quickly gave it a thought and said "No thanks mate, anyway Old Jimmy has been running it and not me!"

According to the bar maid 'Old Jimmy' used to sit there at that very table and drink pints of Scotch when he had an hour or so free. His very own personal table so she said. Well I don't know if I saw something, and I doubt that I ever will. This wasn't a bad bar, it had character but sadly it's since been demolished and is now a Greggs and a Supermarket!

CHAPTER NINE

Basque Attack

It was a sunny Saturday afternoon. I had a great day with my kids, messing in the garden, playing on the trampoline, the sun shining down in a way more akin to some foreign climbs rather than the North East of England. But time was marching on so I came back into the house, had a shower and started getting ready for work. This was a bit earlier than I thought, and funnily enough if it had been any later what happened in this chapter would not have happened at all. I was kitted up in my uniform and quite early for work, so I decided to go down and see a friend on another door in the same town. I had a good feeling that it would be a good night on the door, but then again, when the sun is shining, the weather is good and I have had fun with my kids, I always feel quite positive and optimistic about what the night would have in store.

So I picked up my trusty sidekick and partner in crime at the time, Jimmy, and rocked up at my mates bar. We went through the customary doorman's handshake routine and I grabbed a coke from the bar. I went to chat to a couple of good mates and old school doormen, Silky & Mark. The jokes were flying around and of course the good natured light hearted insults against each other that make for doorman's banter. Just then, a punter I knew approached us and said "Stu, it's all kicking off in your bar mind" oh here we go, I thought. I told Jimmy to stay where he was and I walked over to see what was going on.

As I started to near the pub where I was to start work at in an hours' time, I saw the manager arguing with a group of lads. The lads looked like a stag group or such like, and the manager was telling them to leave the bar. As I approached to offer my help, out of the corner of my eye I saw a man dressed in only a Basque, stockings and suspenders, walking towards the door of the pub as if he was leaving. It was not a pretty sight I can tell you.. Before I knew what was going on he ran at me, fists flying, and jumped in the air grabbing me by the head to try and take me down. I didn't go down but couldn't get him off either. I swung him around with as much force as I could muster and ended up throwing him across a table knocking over and smashing several glasses.

With anticipation thick in the air the bar fell silent as all eyes were on me. I ran over to the bloke in the women's underwear, all the time hoping he was a stag and not a tranny, and grabbed him to throw him out of the pub. This is when the proverbial shit hit the fan. All of his mates were running out towards me, one of them a giant of a man about 6ft 6, made like 'brick shithouse' jumped me from behind getting me in a choke hold. The sheer size and weight of him pushed me to the floor, he was still on my back trying his best to choke me out, but all I was thinking was if I get put to sleep he will kill me. His friends were all running riot now punching and kicking me when I heard the shout of a familiar voice. Jimmy who came up anyway even when I told him that I would be fine by myself, and let me tell you I was bloody pleased that he did! At this point I was feeling that I was not far from losing consciousness, his mates still kicking and punching me.

All of a sudden I felt myself being pulled backwards, which turned out to be the force of Jimmy trying to pull the big fucking ugly giant off my back, which wasn't working. He was still trying to choke me out and I was still trying my very best not to go to sleep, all the while trying to defend myself from punches and kicks, lashing out where I could. From the peripheral vision to my right, I saw another bloke running over and to stop myself from the pending attack, I managed to lash out with my right hand and punch him. He flew back and hit the wall, came back again, and again the same, BOOM. A third time he came back this time too quick for me to throw a punch so I made a grab for him, heard the ripping of material, and ended up with a handful of buttons and a long piece of snapped black wire. I realised it was the bar manager and the wire was the earpiece that I had just wrenched from him.

All of a sudden the immense pressure from around my neck that was making it more and more difficult to breath began to become less and less. I heard the big fella on my back scream out "Arrrrrrrrrrrrrgggh you bastard!" I managed to get out from underneath him to see Jimmy pulling him back with his fingers in his eyes, and then as if out of nowhere the police came running into the bar. The big bloke turned and ran through the bar and managed to escape out of the back fire exit. The bloke in the Basque was arrested. I have got to say the funniest sight that I have ever seen was the bloke sitting in the back of a police van, handcuffed with the cage door locking him inside, sitting there in his black Basque, stockings and suspenders.

When things had calmed down I noticed that the back of my coat was ripped all the way down. 'For fucks sake!' I thought to myself 'that's just new as well!' As I took it off and checked it I felt a cold shiver run down my spine as I realised that my coat wasn't ripped. It had been cut, perfectly cut all the way down the back with something very sharp.

Jimmy told me that the big bloke had pulled out a Stanley knife and ran it all the way down my back, and that was the reason that he put his fingers in his eyes to get him off me. The police managed to catch up with him and arrested him a little later, but just as you would expect, he had no knife on him. So somewhere in the bottom of a drain no doubt sits a Stanley knife slowly rusting away, not to use any more. It turned out that this was indeed a stag night and the bloke in the women's underwear was the stag, the big bloke with the knife, well he was the father in law to be. It makes you wonder doesn't it, what the fuck will happen to the stag a few years down the line, if he ever upsets the big bloke with the Stanley knife's daughter?

It doesn't bear thinking about. The amount of knives being carried on people in this day and age is frightening. Many say they carry them for protection and would never use them, but if it's there and something happens in the heat of the moment, especially when full of drink or drugs, or both, do you really think that they wouldn't use it?

CHAPTER TEN

Following in my Father's footsteps?

Yeah my Dad was a doorman too, so is that why I have gone into the business? Following in my father's footsteps? Well no not quite. My Dad was a very different type of doorman to me, the details are sketchy as for a variety of reasons we don't get on and have not spoken now for 13 or 14 years, so this is what I remember from when I was a kid of about 9 or ten years old. He was quite a well know character my old man, all over the North East but in particular North Shields, Tynemouth and Whitley Bay. He was an old school hardman! He was when I was born, in the Merchant Navy and then went to sea as a Twarlerman and then got into the pub trade for a few years.

This I don't think was the right trade for him, always a very heavy drinker, with the shortest of fuses and the badest of tempers. When my parents divorced and the pub they owned was sold & for a time he went on the door again, having previously done short stints over the years at a variety of places, but the one I can recall was a club called 'Surfers' set in the historical old Plaza building that stood proud at the top of the beach at the Long Sands in Tynemouth. Anyway as I said he went back on the door for a period of time at the Victoria in Whitley Bay, I remember a couple of times being shoved at a table in the corner with a bottle of coke, and bag of crisps. I hated it! This was now at my reckoning 31 years ago, as I remember he was working there a few months and drinking heavily at the time and most likely when he was on the door, most likely, almost certainly more like.

Again forgive me if the details are sketchy but this is from memory three decades ago, at closing time one night there were two off duty firemen from the Firestaion that once stood next door to the Victoria, the two firemen were drunk and at the end of the night were the only two left in the bar. My Dad told them to drink up and leave and they gave him a load of verbal and an argument ensued, now at this point I have been told two different stories and I don't know which is true.

One story is that one of the Firemen picked up his glass smashed it and tried to glass my Dad, the other is that it was a heated argument and a fight started when he tried to eject them from the bar, either way it doesn't change what came next, if it was an attempted glassing or whether it was a struggle trying to eject the two by all accounts my Dad lost his temper, remember the short fuse and the terrible temper I told you about earlier? Well when it goes it really goes and he basically beat the living shit of them both with one of them, as I recall from all of those years ago, ending up with some kind of head injuries. Straight away he must have realised he had went too far and had it on his toes? to a hotel owned by a friend of his a couple of streets away on the Esplanade where he sat at the bar with his friend, the owner, drinking until the police eventually came for him, as he handed over the keys for his classic Mercedes for his friend to look after he knew he was going down.

I won't ever forget the day I found out, it was a Saturday and I was supposed to get one of the infrequent visits from my Dad where no doubt he would have took me to the Vic, sat me in the corner with a coke and stood and got pissed with his cronies and then when he remembered I was there sent me home in a taxi, anyway on the Saturday morning I was at Tynemouth boating lake with my fishing net, I never did get any bloody fish in there, and my mam came down and talked to talk to me.

Now the difference is between my parents is that my mam was, and still is the nicest, kindest, sweetest person that you could imagine and as she told me that he was in prison I could see it in her eyes, it was tearing her apart. Not for her but for what it was doing to me. I won't ever forget that. I am not sure how long he was sentenced to but off to Durham jail he went and got out about a year later, the only contact was one lousy letter with HMP stamped on the front, oh and his bloody TV appearance on a local news and current affair program supporting a friend of his who was a very good boxer and was training in Jail. Yes, that was a lovely day at school after all my mates saw it.

So really to be honest, what I am getting at is I am not following in his footsteps, I am different kind of doorman all together than him, and he isn't the reason that I got into it, it's not something that I ever really wanted to do I just sort of fell into it, but to this day I will have someone in the bar that recognises me as his son and you can see what the think, sometimes they say it, but I am not the same, never have been never will be. Thankfully as the years pass it happens less and less.

It did mind you lead to one quite funny night when chucked a bloke of a bar and he stood outside mouthing off like they do and starting making threats like they do, and he came out with "I am going get you shot you fucking baldy cunt", and then he started name dropping and guess who he was going to ring to get me shot? Yup you guessed it my Dad! I couldn't stop laughing and said to him between chuckles, "No bother mate when you speak to him tell him he owes me 20 years of Birthday and Christmas presents".

But what scares me, and I mean really scares me, my middle son Luca is the loveliest kindest intelligent beautiful kid, he really is, he is 9 years old now and since he was around 6 he keeps saying he want to be a Bouncer like dad. Over my dead body! He is my boy and it's a wicked horrible world sometimes on the doors and I think the dangers are becoming more and more prevalent with the advent and increases in drug related crime and especially knife crime. I have been lucky, so far, over the years and have only received two injuries, I was glassed and ended up with a really deep cut on my head about an inch and a half long and ended up with a lovely scar, and I was bottled but the bottle didn't break as it was smashed down on to my skull over and over again and I have been left with a permanent dent in my skull the same shape as the bottle. But I don't want my boys, any of my boys going into this line of business!

I did once catch him with his school uniform on, my black door tie, earpiece and my badge on his arm standing at the front door, while it

The Diaries of a Doorman

made for a great photograph and we laughed about it, it also scared me and kept me awake most of the night.

Luca, please don't follow your father's footsteps!

I really don't want any of my three amazing sons following in mine!

CHAPTER ELEVEN

Bit of a Let-down

So we all know these days that door staff need to have a licence and to obtain this they must do some mandatory training with an accredited body, reach a certain standard, pass CRB checks etc. This is all laid down by the SIA (Security Industry Authority). But what was it like before this? Well back in the day you didn't need anything, just maybe the ability to 'handle yourself', and sometimes loose morals.

Later came licencing in its early form, ran by the local council. In some way, this may well have been a good idea, but my god, what a complete an utter palaver. I hadn't been working for a while and I decided to get back into the game. In order to do this I needed a licence, so I applied to the local council and submitted all of the numerous documents, photographs and proof that is required. As I queued up at the office, surrounded by taxi drivers waiting to renew hackney cab and private hire licenses, I remember thinking to myself, 'what have I let myself in for?'

This was an odd time in my life, odd maybe isn't the right word, but I don't know how else to describe it. On one hand my step dad, who had been more of a Dad to me then my own, was dying of cancer, and on the other hand the amazing lady that would one day be my wife, was expecting out first baby together; my amazing son Ben. So was I biting off more than I could chew? I was trying to help care for John, my step dad, and support my mother who was caring for him. As well as supporting my wife to be Nicki through the pregnancy of our first son. Well off I went and somehow I managed to fit it all in. Monday to Thursday for 4 hours each night at the local council office, well I am not quite sure what I was expecting, but this most defiantly wasn't it.

The Diaries of a Doorman

It was a joint initiative from local councils and the police. The first night we just more or less sat there, had to introduce ourselves, then the course facilitator from the council introduced himself and talked at length about what we would expect over the course of the week. He explained that there would be input from the police, fire brigade and the ambulance service, as well as others from the local council. To top it all off we had a two part exam to look forward to on the Friday, at this, one lad muttered loudly "Fuck that I am not at bastard school anymore" got up and walked out, slamming the door.

The next night we had the fire brigade who entertained us with some of the most horrific stories and photographs that you could ever imagine with regard to fires in licenced premises. Just about each one he pointed out was over capacity or had the fire exits locked, or both. There we some bloody horrific photos that he showed us, really bad. Then we went off for a coffee break followed by an hour of discussing which fire extinguishers were used for different types of fires. We then spent the next half an hour playing with some real extinguishers in the car park, with some pretty dodgy results.

A lad called Mark who would be about 20 years old, 6ft 5" of muscle, and seemed to be more full of steroids than 'Ivan Drago' in Rocky IV; had been pushing around and taking the piss out of a much smaller bloke aged about 40. He was really taking the piss and giving him as much grief as he could. We didn't know at the time, but this turned out to actually be his father. They had by all accounts fallen out over something and nothing some years before and this is the first time that they had seen each other in about three or four years. We went into the car park and supervised by a member of the fire brigade we all had a go of each of the different types of fire extinguisher. When this was over most people stayed outside to have a smoke before the next part. Well the bloke from the fire brigade left the extinguishers outside didn't he!

So father picks up the water extinguisher and squirts his big galloon of a son and tells him that he is no son of his. The son, shocked and dripping wet, and also devoid of even the slightest bit of brain comprehension; picked up the C02 extinguisher with his huge massive hands, which more than likely could have crushed the black metal cylinder and squirted it towards his dad who ran inside and shut the door. As the massive noise of the extinguisher being discharged echoed in the courtyard of the car park, we couldn't see anything for a second as it squirted, but then we heard a scream.

Despite all of the safety warnings, and there were at least five or six, Mark the big dumb fuck had his left hand half way down, wrapped around the cylinder. He had actually frozen his hand to it. We tried to pull it off for him, but it was just ripping the skin from his hand. He was screaming. When the fire officer returned, he took one look, shook his head and called an ambulance. That was the last that we ever saw of both Mark of his Dad.

The next night was first aid, and that all passed off without anything really, apart from one lad getting his cock out at the front of the room and sticking it in 'Annie's', I think the dummy was called, mouth. He was shouting "go on suck it Annie!" while pissing himself with laughter. The rest of the room sat there, hiding their faces in embarrassment, shock and disgust, depending on who you looked at. Funnily enough he was asked to leave the course. The next night was more interesting, this was with the Police, and for the first two hours they simply showed CCTV of fights in pubs and clubs in Whitley Bay, a tired seaside town that was a low rent, smaller version of Blackpool on a bed day at best. The funny thing was, not one of us in the room didn't know at least one person in the footage, be they doorman or crazy punter. There was some good entertaining stuff on there.

Next thing the police pulled out evidence bags with varying contents for us all to have all look at. So one by one, the evidence bags rustled as they were pulled out of a hold all. First up, a rusty old 9mm handgun, then a bag of mixed ammunition, a couple of different styles of knives, a small bag of coke, a small bag of speed, a small bag of MDMA, a somewhat larger bag of differently stamped Ecstasy tablets, a bag of Heroin and a sheet of LSD tabs.

They were all passed around the group for us to look at, and a few questions were asked of the police. Then the group passed everything back, well not entirely everything, the bag of E's was only half the size that it was when it was brought out. Straight away the rather annoyed copper noticed and said "Come on then who's the clever fucker that nicked some cowies?" We all looked at each other and nobody said anything, the copper asked the same thing getting more and more pissed off each time; nobody owned up to it. He threatened us with arrest, and that still didn't do it. One of us had pocketed a load of pills and I knew it wasn't me, but didn't know who it was.

So the copper was sitting there, absolutely seething, and then he says "OK then, I am going to go out of the room, I am going for a piss and when I get back if the pills are back on the table nothing more will be said." As we all looked at each other accusingly e stood up, stomped out, and almost slammed the door off its hinges. We heard him stomping up the passage, and seconds later, with the scraping of chair legs on the floor and the bang of a fire exit being kicked open a young lad about 18, scruffy little git he was too, bolted out of the fire exit.

We all ran to the fire exit and looked out and see him face down on the floor with a copper sitting on top of him and another one cuffing him. Obviously they were waiting just outside to see if anyone ran. What a complete mug this kid was! He could have even had a chance of getting away with it! Well that led us very nicely into home time, with the prospect of two exam papers to sit the following night.
So exam night came and went with two multi-choice question papers which, well for lack of a better way to put it, weren't exactly rocket science. I had an hour and 40 minutes to complete and check the paper, and like at school in exams we were told to read through the papers first, complete them and then re-check at the end. Once we were finished we could leave the room as that was the completion of the course.

So I sat there and opened the paper expecting, well a hell of a lot more than what was on there, and twenty minutes later found myself leaving the room. I was massively disappointed at the whole course. I can honestly say hand on heart that I didn't learn a single thing;

apart from maybe that it wasn't a good idea to hand drug samples round in class. This was a huge let down from start until finish. A week or so later my test results came through with 100% pass mark, along with my certificate and two badly laminated badges. One was to be worn and the other to be handed to the manager of a venue when you worked a shift. It was suggested that they be kept in the till. Somehow I just expected so so much more…..

CHAPTER TWELVE

The 'Goodfellas' Party

Back a lot of years ago now, I was asked by a mate of mine to do a bit of door work for him, it was a private party he told me, for select VIP's, well I had an idea of what I thought it might be like as my mate shall we say was err, sort of a 'wrongun' as you would a bit 'dodgy' well that was the understatement of the year, but I had known him for a very long time and he didn't get me involved in 'that' sort of thing, he was very well known in certain circles and considered somewhat a villain. The party was set to happen in a weeks' time at a small hotel with a decent size bar and function room and they had hired the whole hotel for their group, every single last part of it, all they wanted me to do was to stand on the door for half an hour between 7.30pm and 8pm and check people against a guest list, and nobody, but nobody would be allowed in if they were not on the guest list, and the wage for this half an hours graft, well £200 for half an hour or so's work is not to be sniffed at so against my better judgment I said yes.

So I am ready and in place for 7.20pm and about 15mins later the big flash cars start turning up outside, and out the guests came, just looking at the guest list it was like a who's who of the local underworld, a few of them I knew myself and many more I knew from the pages of the newspapers, now at this point I am sure you will agree it wouldn't be sensible for me to name names, I happen to like my knee caps just where they are thank you very much! So, no problems everyone was on the guest list, and just one person didn't make it, so as instructed at exactly 8pm I was to lock the doors, my mate told me that I could come in then I join the party if I wanted, so I thought why not, might as well while I am here, but beforehand I went through to the small private bar area and got myself a bottle of becks, always my favorite tipple and sat back and relaxed for a while, I hadn't had much sleep the night before as I was working late at a club and before I knew it I had nodded off to sleep.

Stu Armstrong

By the time that I woke up and went through to the function room they partygoers had just finished the meal and were being entertained by an ex Newcastle United Footballer, who again shall remain nameless. He was cracking some filthy jokes and had all these blokes, dressed in formal black tie, absolutely pissing themselves laughing. When I looked around some were smoking, somewhere drinking very large brandies and some had their heads down towards the table, it was then that I noticed that each table had a plate in the middle of it with what I can only describe as a large pile of white power on it, and by the way it was being snorted I presumed that it was cocaine, not my thing never was, never will be.

So I take up a seat near to the bar with a couple of other lads and the other doorman, and just catch the end of the ex-Newcastle United player cracking dirty jokes or after dinner speaking as they call it, looking at him he was off his tits as well, but hey ho, who knows his eyes may have always been that big! Next up comes of all things a hypnotist, not sure why but I just didn't expect to see a hypnotist here, but here he was. As a round of applause started as he climbed up on stage he looked nervously about the crowd, I don't think that anyone had mentioned the clientele to him when the gig was booked, nervously around the crowd did I say? Nah he was out and out fucking shitting himself to say the least, which did make me snigger to myself.

So before he starts one of the guests, I am presuming the person that arranged it all (Again, no names I like my knee caps just where they are thanks!) stands up and shouts "How, Hypono boy you cunt!", which just made him even more reminisant of Casper the friendly ghost, "You know you're not getting paid if you don't put the 'Heeby jeebies on one of my mates don't you". Well the poor bugger the whole room just fell about laughing at him as he stammered out "Er OK, Er No problem".

Then the show began and I felt a bit sorry for him now, talk about working under pressure! He has a not so glamorous assistant with him in the shape of a little fat kid about 20, who was standing with a small set-up of DJ equipment to one side of the stage, the lights went down, the music started and on with the show! So with '2001 a space odyssey' playing in the background, he ladled the cheesiness out like a giant ball of Edam rolling down the hill at double glouster! "We will be the first brave volunteer" he calls out over the Microphone, "You're the fucking brave one son" someone in the audience shouts out, with the redness in his cheeks building into full flush he calls out again "Come on who will be brave enough, who has what it takes", just when I thought he was on a losing battle someone stands up.

As he walks to the stage he had that certain pallor color about his face, the one that just oozes that he has just got out of jail in the last few days after a lengthy stretch, now I did know the bloke but the lad sitting next to me the other doorman tells me he is just out of a ten stretch for armed robbery, and in fact only got out the day before. I thought to myself, 'so within 48 hours he has went from the exclusive fashion line from HMP, to a dinner suite and black tie, but of a turn up for the books'

So as the armed robber gets up on stage he loves it, all the lads chanting and shouting and cheering and clapping, by far this was the most attention that he had received in the last ten years, probably since he was on crime watch! (If he was). So up he gets onto the stage and 'Hypno Cunt' as everyone is now calling him starts talking to him, he asks his name and the guy says "Fuck off you mug I am not helping you", again the red flush returns to 'Hypno Cunts' face and he says, "OK, I am going to call you Bond, James Bond". Everyone laughs and then "Hypno Cunt" asks for silence and he talks to 'James' and gives it all of his spiel, over and over, over and over and tells him that one day he will have a license to kill. Well you can just imagine the audience all shouting, "I want one as well mate".

Then came the moment of truth, he snapped his fingers, and………………………………………………….and nowt! Not a bloody sausage. "Well everyone I am sorry this thing is a gift it doesn't always work, if this kind gentleman can go back to his seat please we can carry on with the show", with a chorus of Boo's and "Your Shite Hypno Cunt" the armed robber goes back to his seat. Just as he sits down the booming theatrical voice booms over the

Stu Armstrong

Microphone "007 you now have a license to kill", and as that we said the armed robber stood up bolt upright and made a pistol shape with his hands and started looking all over the room, I presume for bloody goldfinger of some fucker, well the lads just all fell about laughing, the room was in hysterics, one lad shouted out "Hey, Hypno Cunt you're not bad"

Almost ruffling with the applause, and I think the feeling that he might just make it out of here alive he seemed to want to better himself, and shouted "007, come on you can do better with you license to kill" with that he mimicked throwing the pistol away with his hands, and what happened next nobody saw coming, let me tell you it funny now, but not on the night. He slips his right hand into the left side of his dinner jacket and pulls a handgun, a bloody real one as well and runs across the room jumps up onto the bar and pretends to stalk his prey. Each time he turned we were all running the other way, or ducking down behind tables just in case he decided one of us was gold finger.

The bloke sitting on the other side of me says to me and other doorman "Go on then lads your meant to be the bouncers for fucks sake put him out or take the shooter of him", "No fucking way mate I replied, I clocked hours ago" I said, with my mate shouting out "No fucking chance mate", the next thing he jumps down from the bar and goes running, like bloody Lindford Christie he crosses the room in a split second and jumps up onto the stage with one easy bound and grabs "Hypno Cunt" by the head, forces him down and puts the gun to his head.

You could hear a pin drop in the room, not a bloody sound apart from the sniffles and sobs coming from Hypno Cunt, 'Shit was he going to shoot him I remember thinking, bollocks I don't want to see this', the next thing 'Bond, James Bond' started to piss himself laughing, a real belly laugh, almost like the laughing policeman and said, "Well then bonny lad, you didn't reckon on that then did you!" It turned out he had just made it all up and played along, never Hypnotized for one second, it also turned out that 'Hypno Cunt' didn't get paid either, maybe because he just fled the hotel straight away!

I don't know if it's true or not but I heard that the Hypnotist never did another stage show from that day on, and 'James Bond', is sitting out a life sentence in some small African republic something to do with trying to rub diamonds worth tens of millions from a diamond mine, and managing to take out four of five guards before one shot him. Maybe he was lucky that it was meant to be a flesh wound, maybe he wasn't. Life in an African jail, don't know about you but I think I would rather be dead myself!

CHAPTER THIRTEEN

Bouncing in the Sun

So, you know what it's like, you go on Holiday with your mates, you have a great time and more often than not at one point or another you turn round and say, "I would love to just quit my job and move over here". Sometimes some bar owner will say something like "Oh my friend you are my very favorite customer, why don't you come live here and work for me?", that's because they're all basically full of shit.

Well that's just what I did, I had a great 2 weeks in Tenerife and I was offered a job, doing PR on a bar. I didn't think all that much about it until I had been home a few days. First thing one cold damp, drab English UK morning I got to work for my day job, which at the time was in a large DIY store, and I thought 'You know what fuck it'. I got home from work that night and went straight onto teletext to price up flights back to the very place that I was less than a week ago, this was long before the days of the 'Interweb' and other such wonders of the technological world.

So, I found a cheap flight, rang up and booked it. A surge of excitement rushed through me the following morning when I walked into work and straight into the manager's office, at the time the manager was a bloke named Fred, who looked and acted like the bastard love child of Adolf Hitler and Basil faulty. My god what a complete and utter tosser he was, and I dare say he still is. His head firmly jammed up his own arse and to add insult to injury he was from Sunderland! Anyway, I digress, I strutted into the manager's office, yeah, that's a pretty accurate description I strutted not walked or even ran into his office. I told 'Fred the Head' that he could firmly go stick it right up his jacksie, accompanied with the obligatory letter of resignation.

The Diaries of a Doorman

Dear Fred,

It is with great disappointment, blah blah blah, tender resignation blah blah blah and so on and so forth, I am giving you the required contractual notice, blah blah jabber jabber and Fred, you a complete dick!

So a couple of weeks later I was off, from Newcastle Airport to Tenerife. As the plane took off I was getting more and more excited about the long summer holiday that my life was going to be; the sun, the sea, the sand and the women! Oh yes this was the life. My mind was racing at 1000 miles per hour and the plane soaring at 15,000 feet was truly a heavy combination. By the time we got up into the sky and levelled off enough to take off the seatbelts I must have nodded off. The next thing that I knew a stewardess, and a pretty nice looking one at that, woke me by gently shaking my shoulders and saying "Sir, Sir, excuse me Sir please wake up and sit up for landing". I must have jumped or something because when I eventually came round everyone was looking at me and the stewardess was saying, between her gritted teeth, to stop herself laughing "I am so sorry Sir, I didn't mean to startle you". No wonder they were all staring at me as I was more than likely dribbling and farting in my slumber in the sky.

As we began the decent into the Airport, all you could see was acres and acres of black, nothing else, and nothing to break the black blanket of darkness. I looked out of the window, until a small twinkle of light far off in the distance appeared, it got bigger and bigger and joined by more and more lights every second. 'Here I am' I thought to myself, here I was the start of an all year long summer that was about to begin, or so I thought anyway. By the time the plane touched down, taxied to a standstill and the doors opened, I was about ready to burst. 'Just let me out of this fucking plane will you' I thought to myself as we waited, and waited, and waited and waited some more for the doors to open. When they finally did I just wanted to get off that plane! I wanted to start my new life. Not get herded around like a herded of mangy, aids ridden, one legged Spanish cows onto the busses from hell, as I always called that shuttle bus from the plane to the terminal building. You know the ones I mean, if there is say 100 passengers on the plane they heard

98 of them onto a bus, packed so tight that the windows are littered with little squashed up piggy looking faces, bang up against the windows and doors.

Obviously the empty bus behind it wouldn't open its doors until this one was full, oh no. So the second bus managed to get on the remaining two passengers. At the airport terminal, I pushed and shoved and made sure that I was first into the building and first through to the baggage hall. I grabbed my rucksack and rushed out of the airport, jumped into a taxi, and off I went to Los Cristianos. I wanted to be in Los America's but I had a mate in Los Cristianos who offered to put me up, at a crappy Lille bedsit that he rented over a bar called 'The Stumble Inn'. All was sounding good, and it would've been if I ever made it there. At that point I had no idea whatsoever that I would only be in the bloody country for about 6 hours!

For some reason, probably because it's a bit further from the airports, the taxi driver took me Los Americas, as we pulled up on the strip outside an open aired nightclub called 'Mrs T's' I realised where I was. I complained to the driver and he kept saying "No, No Americas, America you pay you pay". I tried until I was blue in the face to explain, but he didn't care, he wanted to get back to the airport for another foreign mug. 'Well pal' I thought to myself 'you are not taking me for a ride'. Well I suppose he already had as I had rode in his taxi all the way from the airport! So I told him that I wasn't going to pay, jumped out grabbed my rucksack from the boot and off I went.

Not really worrying too much about the taxi ordeal, I thought I would have a pint or two and grab some food then get a taxi along to Los Cristianos. So there I was, sitting outside a bar, I can't for the life of me remember its name, when I heard a loud shout in Spanish. I looked around and there was the taxi driver at the other side of the road with the Guardia Civil, one of the two police forces out there. It is easy to spot which are which, as the Policia Locale dress in blue uniforms and the Guardia in green. 'Shit!' I thought 'I can't be doing with this they won't listen to a word I say!' So with a hasty slurp of San Miguel, I picked up my rucksack and ran around the back of the bar which led directly to the beach, as I glanced behind me the taxi driver and his green pals were still trying to cross the road. I made it down the stairs and onto the beach in record time, mainly because I tripped down the stairs. Without time to dust myself off I ran along the beach, stumbling and slipping in the sand with the weight of my stuffed rucksack on my back, I could hear the shouts behind me and they seemed to be getting closer.

Just up ahead was a small jetty with a couple of boats around it, one was a decent size speed boat and people seemed to be on-board partying and I could hear not only English accents but Geordie accents! I thought 'well let's give it a go'. I ran up the to jetty and quickly explained what was going on to two lads, one from Wallsend and another from Gateshead. 'Would they help me?' I thought. My heart was beating through my chest as the taxi driver and his greenie meanie chums got closer and closer.

"Quick for fucks sake, jump on!" The kid from Wallsend said, I jumped and the weight from my backpack tipped me backwards banging me head hard onto some water skis lying on the deck. Just then the gnarling sound of the engine started up, the crashing sound of the propeller in the shallow waters and we were away, flying across the water and away from the beach, but more importantly the Guardia. As me and the two lads on the boat got talking I explained my plight and they thought it was hilarious, they told me not to worry and they would drop me further up the coast later on. 'Why not?' I thought, 'it's not as if I was going to get a better offer', unless it was from the Guardia, with a nice cell to sleep in for the night, which I seriously didn't fancy sharing with loads of cockroaches and got only knows what else! Actually did you know that only female cockroaches can fly? That's a crappy fact for you but there you go.

So there I was, skimming across the waves at Godspeed when the vodka came out. A nice bottle of Absolut, and before long we were all completely shitfaced, mortal, stinky rat-arsed drunk, god only knows how the boat wasn't flipped. At some point I fell asleep and when I woke up we were drifting with the other two lads snoring their heads off as well. I quickly woke up, Gary the lad from Gateshead that was sailing the boat. When he realised where we were he nearly shit himself. No maps, no charts, no GPS, no radar, no fucking nothing.

"Don't worry mate" he said, "My Granda was at sea during the war so it's in my blood, I will just navigate from the stars". Well he was that pissed I am surprised he could even stand up never mind steer the boat. He began telling me a story about when this happened before and how they found their way back, 'Before?' I thought, 'shit. this is a right dip-shit here', but still, they had saved my skin.

It would seem that a few weeks back when this had happened they were boarded by the Spanish coastguard who chased them briefly in a high powered clipper, that's the boat type not the lighter, and then they jumped on board with guns drawn. It would seem that the smuggling of drugs from Morocco, which is not far away, was rife, but after a full hour long search of them and the boat they were told to follow them back to port to find their way home.

Well the vodka and the day's events were catching up on me and I have no idea how long I had been asleep for. When I woke up with the sun burning down on my face we were tied up in a small harbour of sorts. Where were my two new mates then? Nowhere to be seen. 'Well bugger this for game of soldiers' I thought and got off the boat and climbed a few steps onto the street. After a few yards, I sat down in a small local café', ordered some water and some strong coffee. I was only a few yards from the boat but because there were a few steps up from the harbour and the boat lay low in the water I couldn't see it, and couldn't see the Geordie Duo walking back to the boat, jumping on board and setting off.

I heard the engines and saw them shooting off into the beautiful blue sea, quickly becoming a spec on the horizon, 'Ah well never mind' I thought as I sipped my coffee and asked a waiter where I was as I none of this looked familiar to me at all after numerous trips to Tenerife over the years. "Maspolomas, senior" he said. I had never heard of the place so I asked him where the next big town was, he looked at me strangely like I was an idiot because I didn't know where I was and replied "Playa Del Ingles, Senior'".

"SHHHHHIIIIIIITTTTTTT" At that point I did know where that was, oh yes, it was only in bloody Gran Caneria wasn't it! They had only stopped on another Island and left me asleep, and I had got up and wandered off and they had left me, 'great' I thought, 'just bloody great'.

So I walked the few miles into "Playa Del Ingles", famed for things such as, its nudist beach and its impressive array of sand dunes which were used in many films including Star Wars, Indiana Jones and the Clint Eastwood spaghetti westerns along with many others. Apart from that I knew nothing else about the place, well, apart from that it was hot as fuck and I thought I was going to die of heat exhaustion with vodka sweating from my pores!

As I started to hit the outskirts of 'Playa Del Ingles' the main resort on that side of the winter sun island, things became busier and busier and busier. Up to the right there seemed to be a hive of activity on the side of the road, people shouting and screaming with banners and placards. I had no idea what they said or what they were chanting and shouting but that obviously believed in whatever it was. As more and more police turned up, more protesters followed and before I knew it I was caught up in the midst of all this. The police started herding everyone backwards towards a field, presumably to get them out of the street, I thought to myself, 'Bollocks, I have had enough excitement for one day'. More and more people were being pushed back by the police, not the Guarda this time but the blue uniforms of the tamer Polica Locale, so off I went, not hanging round.

Maybe I shouldn't have ran, then maybe I wouldn't have ran into the big ugly Spanish chief copper, well that what he looked like, with gold bits all over have uniform! Maybe that was my first mistake but maybe not, who knows, what a bastard this fella was! He was mouthing off to me 50 to the dozen and the only word that I could make out was 'Bastard' but more like "Bastardo Bastardo", cheeky fucker! So after he told me the same thing about five times and looked at me for an answer, I shook my head, opened my hands and said 'English, mate speak English' to which his reply was "Pah Bastardo English Pigs" and he actually spat onto the floor as he said this, cheeky bastardo he was!

Still getting nowhere I turned around and started walking away from him, bad move I bet your thinking? Well you could would be right as he grabbed me by the shoulder and spun me around. He pulled me so close to his face that the pungent stench of his breath was almost overwhelming, I wish that I could describe it as anything, even garlic but I can't, but just thinking about this all those years ago makes me want to heave. This big Spanish dude had the worst case of shitbreath that I had ever known and when he started bellowing at me, right in my face, it made it even more pungent, making me want to wretch, and that was my welcome to the town that was destined to by my home for few months.

Luckily for me the crowd that were being pushed back into a field decided that they didn't want to go and started kicking off big style. Stones, bottles, you name it started getting thrown by the fifty or so scruff bags protesting. Spanish big wig bad breath, shouted something at me and flapped his hand if as if to tell me to sling my hook, and slung my hook I did, no I wasn't piss farting about I had had enough, I was fucked, totally and utterly Donald Ducked!

Across the road was a big, but rather odd looking complex, part shopping centre, part bars, restaurants and nightclubs. The closest one to me was a small bar up a set of dodgy concrete steps that went up the side of the building, so up I went, still dragging my now very much worse for the wear rucksack up behind me. At the top of the stairs a strange sort of bar presented its self to me, a big black sign inside with a bright green bat in the middle and the words 'Spook Bar' emblazoned underneath. The bar was on the second floor and bizarrely it was half open air and half covered. It seemed to be open but nobody was behind the bar, I knocked on the bar counter a few times, there was only a handful of customers in at this point, I shouted a few times into an open door behind the bar and nothing.

By this time I was ready to just collapse with tiredness as I stood there like a bloody scarecrow I could see, and smell, a pot of coffee bubbling away behind the bar. I went behind the bar and was just about to pour myself a coffee planning on paying the bar owner when he returned, when I felt an arm on my shoulder, "Hey, what time is this to arrive? You are two days late, hope you start work now?". I must have looked puzzled as he said more or less the same thing again and this time I thought to myself 'Hello, this bloke thinks I am his new staff member that obviously hadn't turned up!' Well I needed a job if was going to find anywhere to live so I just said "Yes sorry I am late, the plane had troubles", to which he laughed and said "Fucking planes, they always trouble, trouble trouble trouble, I never ever fly, I refuse".

So there I was, thinking this could be a canny little job working behind this bar, stress-free, plenty tips, so off I went to and as the bar got busier I got more and more tired, but the money was getting its self in. At about 1pm he said to me 'OK, you go home, you sleep start back tonight a 9pm, you don't be late again and no aeroplanes'.

This bloke, who I had managed to find out was called Havier, certainly didn't like planes. So I told him I had nowhere to stay and he gave me an address and a map of some apartments about ten minutes' walk away. Off I went and I found it pretty quickly, it looked, how shall we put this………Like a complete fucking shithole. Oh and to get to it you had a take a foot bridge over 6 lanes of busy motorway. So over I went, I noticed of all things Brazilian flags hanging out of at least of third of the windows of this huge block. When I inquired, they told me they had one bedsit type left, a week's rent in advance and the keys could be mine, I can't exactly remember how much it was but I remember thinking it was stupidly cheap. I was then asked in broken English if I was sure I wanted to live here, "All Brazil, All Brazil was two Germans they go not like Brazil people".

Well at that point in my life I honestly didn't think I had met anyone from Brazil, so I thought why not. In I went, sat down, and before I knew it I was sprawled out on the bed and off to the land of nod. I was woken up by the loud bangs of fireworks being set off very close by, at least that's what I thought at the time, as I found out a few days later they were actually gunshots! It seemed as if a lot of my Brazilian neighbors had guns which they would fire off into the sky whilst hanging out of the windows of their rooms if they got pissed or if Brazil were playing football.

Anyway I woke up and it was 8pm, just an hour to get a shower, a change of clothes and grab some food before I started work. I must have been showered and ready quickly, as after running the Gauntlet across the motorway bridge and a ten minute walk I was sitting in a burger joint in the Kasbah by 8.35. The refreshment of the shower and some food made me feel so much better after my weird last two days! So once more up these dodgy stairs that only a few hours earlier I had struggled up, partly with exhaustion and partly because I had been dragging a now knackered ruck sack up. When I walked into the bar Havier seemed to beam that I was there, and shouted right across the now half full bar "Stu, my friend you came back you came back".

He seemed rather shocked to see me to say the least, which was a bit odd. He then explained that the Bouncer wasn't coming in tonight and as I had told him that I had 'Done it bit' in the UK he asked if I would cover. Well I was talking myself into a job and trying to really big up my skills, and my real version of having 'Done a bit' in the UK was quite a bit different to what I had led him to believe, in fact at this point I had worked three days and nights at the Fish Quay festival back home in North Shields. Still the Bouncer got paid around 3 times what the bar staff did so I quickly agreed.

My position was to be anywhere from the pub doorway at the stop of the stairs he explained, to the middle or even bottom of the stairs. All of the smaller bars within the Kasbah complex all only had one Doorman on, but they were all so close, and most of the owners related that really we had a pretty strong team. I became good mates with the Doorman at the next bar, Gaz, a bit of a jack the lad from Manchester. He gave me his story one night, everyone who was working out here seemed to have a story and everyone seemed to be either running away from someone or something, or seeking a new life of winter Sun.

The story my mate Gaz gave me was that he was on the run from Westham's notorious ICF (Inter City Firm) who most people back in England had heard of. They would have a been at the peak of their notoriety when led by Cass Pennant. But something didn't ring true about this as he also told me that he had never been out of Manchester in his life until coming over here, but then I thought to myself you just never know, maybe something had happened at a game in Manchester or something like that. Anyway me and Gaz became closer and closer mates, and would often go for something to eat together after work. We happened to stumble on, of all things, an Indian restaurant, but one with a difference. There was quite a lot of construction work going on the island back in the day and a lot of cheap Asian labour was brought across. Well this was a restaurant basically for them. The first time we stumbled across it, half pissed, we went in we got some very funny looks from the owner, staff, and customers being the only white Europeans in there. The meal was amazing and stupidly cheap because it wasn't for holiday makers, or even locals, it catered just really for the Asian migrant workers. On top of the cheapness the authentic Indian food was amazing, none of your bright red Chicken Tikka Masala shit in here. After ending up there just about every night of the week, both me and Gaz ended up very good friends with the owner Ravi, and his family, and most of the regular punters.

I remember Gaz saying to him, "Any trouble in here, let us know we can sort it out for you" I also remember thinking to myself that Gaz was trying to big us up just a little too much. Ravi's reaction was hilarious and Gaz's face even better. Ravi said "come with me I show you how I deal with trouble, with Lager Louts if they get lost and come here" He took us round behind the small counter come bar area and from underneath pulled a bloody huge knife come machete type thing. The sort of thing that would put Crocodile Dundee right in the shade. Well Gaz just about shit himself when Ravi took a wild swinging motion with the huge knife as if to chop at Gaz's head, Gaz shouted "No Ravi No!" Ravi and me were both pissing ourselves laughing. Safe to say that Gaz didn't try to big us up with our new mate Ravi anymore. One thing that puzzled me in there was this, a lot of the customers had just come over from India, couldn't speak English, were not really westernised at all and they ate in what I was told was a traditional way in the part of India that they came from which was rural and isolated. They ate with their hands, scooping up large handfuls of all kinds of wonderful Indian dishes with chapatti's or just with their hands.

One night me and Gaz were persuaded to give it go, both of us a bit worse for the wear we did, and it wasn't too bad at all. But how the fuck did we have stained hands from the curries for the next week? Nothing, and I mean nothing, would get this stuff off, scrubbing with bleach the lot, yet the regulars and their families who ate like this all the time never had so much a bit of yellow curry stain about them. Anyway as I said we got know Ravi and his family really well and one day he just stopped charging us all together, he told us that we were his friends and guests. This really was a top bloke, who all these years later I am still in touch with, he now lives on the UK not far from Leeds and my god has he come a long way? He has a string of restaurants and even diversified into importing as a wholesaler in bulk Indian cooking ingredients.

I went down to see he him a few years back and his restaurant couldn't be any different from the one in Gran Caneria back in the day, a beautiful, amazing place, with amazing prices to match, bloody expensive amazing prices, but still he wouldn't charge me. Top bloke! It turns out he still has the place in Gran Caneria but the crappy area off to the side of the town was taken over by tourism some years before and its changed a lot. I couldn't believe it when he showed me the photos, one thing Ravi is good at is making money it would seem. He will sell you a quality meal in pleasant surroundings with great service, but fuck me he will have your eyes out when the bill comes for the privilege. Well good luck to him I say.

Anyway after a few minor fights and bits and bobs I was enjoying my job. I had ended up staying on the Door as the lad who I had covered for never ever came back, maybe he fell asleep on a speed boat and was in Tenerife or Lanzarote or somewhere. I will always remember this Saturday night, this was the first time on the Door that I was involved in a naughty, and I mean very naughty mass brawl. About six bars up from where me and Gaz worked, was a bar called 'Fantasy Island' it was one of the busiest most popular bars, a lot of the holiday reps would take people there to start the bar crawls.

I remember standing there and Gaz had gone to what we called the 'Pop Machine' which was like a coke vending machine, but filled with cans of Heineken, to get us yet more cold cans to drink while working. While I was waiting this girl came up to me, she must have been about 19 at the time, that made her only a couple of years younger than me. She was a stunner and seemed to have taken bit of a shine to me. She started chatting and flirting on with me, she was from Northern Ireland, I can't remember her name, but whatever it was she has a gold chain hanging from her rather shapely neck with a small gold frog hanging from it. I said "Is that a frog? Why a frog" and she came out with "Have you seen the advert for Malteasers and the wide mouthed frog", "Yeah" I told her. At the time in the UK an advert was being shown for Malteasers with a cartoon frog with a huge mouth. "Well you know how the frog puts the sweets into his mouth and rolls them around?", "errr yeah" I said starting to think she was a bit nuts, but still she was beautiful and I am always a sucker for a woman with an Irish accent. I had no clue as to what was coming next, "Well I have already asked your boss and know you finish work in ten minutes", which I did, "Take me back to your apartment with you and I will be rolling your balls around my mouth like a wide mouthed frog".

I was quite surprised at this as she didn't seem the type at all, but hey, I wasn't going to look a gift horse in the mouth. So hand in hand we walked over to where Gaz was standing and as it was quiet I had a word and slipped away ten minutes early. Just as we were going to head down the stairs I heard what I can only describe as carnage; shouts, bangs smashing glasses the lot. It was coming from the direction of Fantasy Island, "Wait there" I said to her as both me and Gaz ran round. All we saw were bodies getting thrown around like they were nothing by the Bouncer from Fantasy Island; it looked like a scene from a war movie.

The Bouncer that had worked here for a number of years, I had met him a few times and he was bizarre, in fact more than that. He was one of the biggest blokes I have ever seen in my life, he must have been, and this is a conservative estimate, at least 6ft 8" tall and not kidding you nearly as wide. He was a local whose family had a farm up the coast somewhere, a very poor farm and from what I can gather they didn't bother with a tractor or a horse to move really heavy stuff and equipment, they just used this big dumb lump. He didn't speak a word of English and with IQ levels in the minus figures his native Spanish wasn't so good either. With the size of the lump, with muscles on his muscles and a serious lack of anything even resembling intellect, and a very short fuse, often you would hear that there was a fight in the bar and he would drag two blokes out with ease and then chuck them down the stairs.

Anyway, tonight wasn't his night at all, there must have been about 25 to 30 lads kicking off, and they were all big lumps and all going for him. Yeah he was throwing them around the bar like they were nothing, but he could only do this for so long and there was only the two of us, me and Gaz, that went round to help. I didn't like this guy that much, he had a reputation as a bully and for being unpredictable, I had often thought that the amount of serious violence in this bar may have somehow been fuelled by him. Thinking on my feet unsure of what to do to help this guy, like I said I didn't like him a lot, but a Doorman's and Doorman no matter what colors you wear as the old saying goes. So in my head and my heart I knew I had to do something, there were just too many to try and fight so I ran over the bar that was now devoid of all of the very scantily clad barmaids, vaulted the bar and found a fire extinguisher, jumped back up on the bar and pulled out the pin and squeezed the handles together to deploy it. Nothing! Not a bloody thing.

I looked quickly again behind me and found a black C02 extinguisher, back up on the bar I deployed it in the direction of these mad idiots for a second or so at a time, well I am sure that you have all seen one go off, even if just on TV. When you deploy the C02 it makes one hell of a noise, that was enough to stop them and they were staring at me standing on the bar. I jumped off and kept making quick squirts towards them and that saw them off. Dumb and dumber came over and shook my hand, and the manager of the bar came out from underneath his rock, err I mean out of his office. "That was pretty impressive, do you want to come and work for me?", "No thanks I replied, I already have a job!

I thought the wide mouth Irish bird had gone, then she caught my eye and winked and shrugged as if to say sorry and wandered off hand in hand with some odd lucking blond haired geezer! In my head I decided he was a German, most likely called Herman! "Fucking bastard Germans, bad enough that they nick the sunbeds, tried to shoot my Grandad (But didn't) during the war, and now one's nicking my bird" I said to Gaz, who somehow had a bottle of Vodka from god knows where in his hand that he was sipping from.

Next day I was due to be paid by Spook bar for the week, I had done a shit load of extra shifts on both the bar and the door and was looking forward to the pay packet. I got to the bar at about 12pm lunchtime, they open at 11am but there was always someone there from about 8am. When I got there the shutters were down and it was closed and all locked up with a sign in both Spanish and English that basically said 'No more money, no pay bills I have gone away, you will not find me, sorry'. Oh that's just bloody great I thought, my luck since I left the UK was really bad, but then again it has been all of my life. If I didn't have bad luck then I would have no luck at all!

'What now' I thought to myself, payday was also rent day, only one thing sprang to mind, so I walked the half a dozen or so bars up and into Paradise Island, hmmm just a day after I was offered a job and turned it down on the spot. When I arrived the bar was quiet, they hadn't been open for long and the manager was sitting on the customers side of the bar drinking coffee. He seemed like a pretty decent bloke when I had met him a few times before. He told me he had sold up a couple of bars and moved out some ten years before from Essex, and by god, by the accent alone, you could tell he was from.

So I slid up onto the bar stool next to him, and after exchanging pleasantries I wasted no time and went in for the kill, "This job mate, is it still on offer?" In his nasal Essex accent he said "Yeah, course it is my son but you said you were happy at Spook, what's changed your mind then?" Well I didn't want to crack on that I only wanted to work for him in this mad hellhole because Spook's owner had 'Done a moonlight flit' so I said, "Well Dave, I have thought about it long and hard all night mate, and I want a stepping stone to the top, Spook isn't anywhere near being a stepping stone to anywhere, never mind the top, and obviously everybody knows yours is the bar to be , the best bar in Gran Canaria never mind just the Kasbah" I was really playing up to his ego.

So I got the job, to start that night and it was just over double the money that I was making at Spook, but, and this is a big but, a big 6ft but, the BUFG as people called him 'Big Unfriendly Giant" was staying. I just presumed he would be leaving and basically my job was to work with him and calm him down when he went, and these are Dave's words not mine "Mental Mental Chicken Oriental". "Dave, have you seen the size of him? You do know he speaks no English and I speak no Spanish, how the fuck am I meant to control him, he is a nutter!"

Dave started to laugh and said "Stu, he can speak perfect English he just pretends he can't so he doesn't have to listen to patter from boring punters, and he reckons it scares people, like he isn't scary enough already!" He then let out a long belly laugh, a real laughing Policeman style laugh. "Oh go on then what the hell I said, let's have a go then", "Goodman, Goodman" said Dave. "But one thing mate, can you rock and Roll?, if you can't rock and roll no job". "Rock and bloody roll, Dave what the fuck has that got to do with anything?" I said, "Well I can't dance to save my life but I can sing a bit!" Dave thought this was fun "Rock and Roll Stu mate, not Rock and Roll", Yeah this made sense Dave! "Stu, I mean can you have a ruck, can you handle yourself should you need to?" Now it all clicked into place, or maybe I was just being dozy that day. "Well I am not claiming to be any kind of hard man but I boxed a bit a few years ago and I will stand my ground, if someone goes for you, the Jolly Green Giant or bar staff then you will see me move like a startled gazelle and take them out if I can. I stand my ground and I don't back down". (Bollocks, isn't that a line from a song??)

Anyway Dave smiled and said "You my son now work for me", "Thanks" I said. Funny bloke was Dave, I got the impression that he had a lot of fingers in a hell of a lot of pies, many of these pies were the type of pie that you would get your finger burnt in. As I start walking out of the bar Dave shouted after me "Oi don't treat me like a mug again Stu, you really think that I didn't know the Spook had gone down the pan mate really. I know all everything in this place"

It turned out that he did, how shall we say, some banking services for certain select clientele or I can just say he was a Loan Shark and this is who the money Spook owned belonged to. I always had a feeling that he also laundered dirty money, or drug money through his bar. A Couple of times a day, on the Jolly Green Spanish Giants day off, he would come in with two brief cases, one in each hand and give them to Dave, Dave who obviously also thought that he had a touch of Del Boy chucked in with his Tony Montana act always said "Lovvvvverly Jubbbbbly!" And in that bloody accent it used to get right on my tits.

His office door was always locked when the brief cases went in there but one day he must have forgotten to lock the door. We got on well me and Dave and I used to just wander in and out of his office if I needed to without knocking. If it was locked then he was either up to no good, or had a bird in there with him, sometimes both. I looked through the door and saw more cash on his desk than I have ever seen in real life. Dave's face went bright red. I left the office and shut the door. I have never told anyone about this until now, neither I nor Dave ever mentioned it. But Dave is so obviously not his real name.

So things were going quite well. Any little rucks we sorted out between us, but I did feel a little like I was on Gulliver's travels with this huge monster. I never actually did find out his name. When he lost his temper and decided to run riot like a bald version of King Kong, somehow I seemed to be able to stop him kicking off just in the nick of time. I was paid on time every week, sometimes a day early and sometimes too much. All was going well until one Saturday night about 11pm, peak time for this bar, when we were raided by the police, and I don't mean a couple of coppers coming in this was a full on raid. I would guess at about 100 coppers. All of us were searched, customers, staff the whole lot. Out of the corner of my eye, when they first arrived I think, but can't be sure, I saw Dave trying to make a swift exit, but he hadn't made it and was in the office with the police. There were quite a few arrests for ecstasy as it was the time when it was really big, well I say arrests, by all accounts they got a little slap around and relieved of some of their hard earned holiday cash. The Cowies were taken off them and told no doubt to fuck off.

I have no idea how but Dave had the place open again by the following afternoon like nothing had ever happened. I really did have the feeling that it was the beginning of the end here, but whatever Dave was up to, I liked him, we got on well and we had ended up mates. Maybe he was all good but, well I am saying nothing. Anyway I told Dave I was looking for another job. I am sure if Lurch the Spanish giant got wind of it he would have wanted to come as well, we ended making a really good team, I had him more of less trained to my command, and without any dog treats! Dave didn't want to go, and said to me "You're the only person that I have met that can train and control King Kong over there, and it's not like I can get rid of him is it?", "Why?" I asked him. He looked confused and said "Surely you know Stu, his elderly parents have owned this land for a few generations and actually owned the whole complex, he likes to chuck people about and if I bin him off I will lose the lease on my bar. In fact the parents are very old and quite ill, and he inherits the lot mate, so what can I do to stop you leaving?"

Well after this I don't know whether to believe him or not, so I said to him, more as a piss take than anything else "A car Dave, I need a car", to which he replied straight away "No worries, it won't be new mind!"

So a couple of days later I was shocked when I got to the roundabout outside the Kasbah. There he was, sitting waiting for me in a car that wasn't his Mercedes at the side of the road. As I went over I thought 'Surely not', and then he chucked the keys at me. "All yours mate he said, on the condition if you leave, or leave the island you give me it back". Well I was shocked, back in England I had took my car off the road and left it on my mother's drive, my bright red Fiesta XR2, with the pepper-pot wheels. I loved that car but I had always dreamt of a convertible one day, and that day had arrived. Not a top of the range sports car, but a Renault 19 convertible. I had never even seen a convertible one of these, it was a wreck, rust holding it together but you know what it wasn't too bad to drive, until I lost it, but that's another story!

So that was me stuck working at Paradise Island with my trained giant Spanish half-wit, or so I thought, as a few weeks later Dave came in and just said sorry lads, I am shutting down selling what's left of the lease and going back to England. We were both shocked, really shocked. I always had the feeling that Dave couldn't go back to England for whatever reason but he was gone within a week, he told me he would be back in two months to tie up loose ends and I could keep the car until then. So once again I was out of a job! At the other side of the Kasbah was one of the now famous, but just really building at the time 'Linekers Bars', all of them owned by Wayne, brother of the footballer and Crisp seller Gary Lineker. I wandered in one day and asked for a job. I had been in a few times and the manager knew me by sight. I was surprised that straight of the belt he said, "Yeah mate, if you can start tonight but just for you and not your overgrown trained chimp". Well I felt a bad but I had to take the job, as it turned out King Kong went to Essex with Dave and as far as I know never came back!

Well in the time I worked at Linekers all kinds came out of the woodwork. This wasn't Wayne Linekers bar at all; the bloke that owned it jumped on Wayne's gravy train, stole his idea, stole his concept, and stole his name and even his branding. Even at this point there was a legal case pending with Wayne trying to take the owner to court. This actually went on for years and years. I remember a lot of years after I had come back to the UK, and stopped messing about, in the Sun, reading a newspaper article saying that Wayne Lineker had won substantial damages in court from the bar owner, who if I remember rightly couldn't afford to pay them. He actually sold Wayne the bar at a cheap price to stop himself going bankrupt, so really he scored in the end, bought another bar for his empire very cheap and got paid a lot of money in damages. The bar is still there to this day, only a couple of months ago a good mate of mine, Carl, was over there and checked it out for me.

I worked in Linekers for another few weeks then decided to fly home for a week and see family. I drove to the airport in my Renault convertible ashtray, well Dave's, and parked it up. When I got home I was all set to only stay week, the bar expected me back and so did the people that I rented the apartment off in the Brazilian Hell hole as it was known, but do you know something they were all slightly crackers but I got on really well with them, great people. I guess maybe it's just the Latin temperament that made them a little crazy! When I was home I went to see a friend of mine Malcolm at a bar that he had recently taken over in Gateshead. It was a belting bar, but for some reason he had decided to quit. He was a manager for a large brewery chain of managed houses. It just so happened that when I went over one morning that week, I think it was the Friday, I was due to fly back on the Sunday, that the Area manager from the brewery was there and was more or less begging Malcolm to stay or they would have had to close the bar. He wouldn't. It turned out him and his wife were splitting.

Always the gobshite I piped up, I was brought up living above my parents pubs I can run it with my hands tied behind my back, it was just meant as a joke. Guess what??? An hour later I was the manager of the bar!! I never did go back to Gran Canaria as planned and have always wondered what happed to the Renault 19, was it still there covered in a mountain of sand and parking tickets? Surely not. This was the best part of 20 years ago!

Anyway the pub in Gateshead did well, I started doing food but to keep the overheads low I persuaded my Mam and my Granny to do the cooking and I would microwave it during the week. Well it went down a storm, all apart from the Spaghetti Bolognese, for some reason nobody ever ordered it. So me being me, I took it off the menu, whacked a bit of old cheese on it and stuck it back on the menu as 'Mama Armstrong's Italian Style Pasta', well it bloody flew out they couldn't get enough! So next I added 'Mama Armstrong's Home Made Steak Pies' they flew out as well.

I didn't stay there long. There was something about it that to this day I can't put my finger on that I didn't like about the bar, so I asked the Brewery for a transfer and ended up running the Musketeer in Forrest Hall. I loved that bar I really did. I met for the first time a lad called Mark Lancaster, we have been firm friends ever since and still see him to this day. I loved that bar and regretted leaving to move into I.T. and working the doors off and on at nights. I miss the place.

Just over a year ago, I was out on my Motorbike with a mate of mine Craig on his bike and as we went past my heart sunk, a huge bulldozer with a huge yellow arm and scoop was knocking it down. Gutted I loved that place. It's now an Aldi or a Netto or some other crappy supermarket.

Stu Armstrong

Whitley Bay

Back in the Day

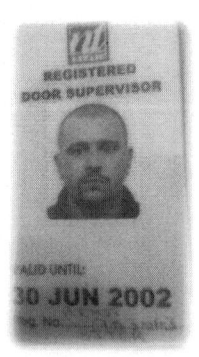

The Diaries of a Doorman

Special Jobs

Learning to Fly

CHAPTER FOURTEEN

The Good, The Bad & the Sad – Written by Ivan 'Doc' Holiday

My name is Ivan 'Doc' Holiday, I am a Canadian bouncer that has lived in the USA for 20 years. I'm a published author of four books on nightclub & bar security. I am accepted worldwide as a leading authority in the field of Nightclub & Bar security today. At 55 years old, I have worked over 100 nightclubs & bars in both Canada and the US, a career spanning 32 years.

I have travelled to England on business trips and in 2009 when I was hired by a large training company to go on tour in the UK and hold three training seminars in London, Birmingham and Manchester.

I met with SIA President Bill Butler & other SIA officials in Coventry at a security convention. I met and spoke at length with Mark Dawes founder of the NFSP LTD, author of the book 'Understanding Reasonable Force' and the SIA's expert on Physical Intervention & Physical Restraint. I attended one of Mr Dawes Physical Intervention training sessions and participated in the class. I also attended and observed the Get Licensed Inc SIA -Door Supervisor training classes. So, let's look at the similarities of the bouncers in all three countries.

Basically in the bouncing trade you will get good bouncers, bad bouncers and sad bouncers. Sad, as in totally fucking terrible. The UK boys call them 'Jacket Fillers'. In Canada they are called 'Posers'. In the USA they are called 'Wannabe Bouncers'. A good bouncer does his job professionally & has the right size, strength, attitude &

brains to get the job done. He is a bouncer who enjoys the trade and takes his job seriously. Next we have the bad bouncer. This guy has a couple of the right traits and the aptitude to do well but prefers to do more of the wrong. He does a half ass job, just enough to get a pay check. He is lazy, selfish, arrogant & ignorant. He says he is a professional bouncer while he acts unprofessionally most of the time.

Then last but not least you have the sad bouncer. A person who is a waste of a pay check and should never have been hired. He does not have the physical traits or mental ability needed to perform the job. Basically he can't even do a half ass job. In the UK, Canada & the USA there are forms of bouncer training. In the UK, you have the SIA that is making an attempt to license, train & regulate Door Supervisors. In a few provinces in Canada you have basic security training programs. For example, in British Columbia a bouncer becomes certified under the Ministry of Public Safety and Solicitor General Office. The course, called 'BST' (Basic Security Training), is a 40 hour program that covers law, customer service, and other issue related to security operation.

In Alberta, bouncers have to take a six-hour 'ProTect' course that teaches staff to identify conflicts before they become violent, and how to defuse situations without resorting to force. Here in the USA, a few states have bouncer licensing with basic Security guard training. But as previously stated, not all provinces and states in the Canada and the USA have mandatory bouncer licensing. There is still a lot of 'Old School' bouncing going on in place here and in Canada. But at least an attempt is being made in some areas to get some type of regulation & training in the bouncing trade.

Now comes a short professional assessment of bouncing in all three countries. In a nutshell: if you take a Good idea and combine it with a Bad system, you get a Sad result.

GOOD

It is good to have the nightclub & bar security trade recognized as a viable professional trade. Have men and women properly trained and licensed is an excellent start. Solid criminal background checks, re-up training & proper monitoring is a step in the right direction. Making club and bar owners accountable for safety of their patrons and educating them is a definite plus.

BAD

You have a lot of 'Old School' bouncing here in the USA and Canada still. With this comes a lot of violent felons and thugs working as bouncers, thanks to the lack of club owner education & zero criminal background checks. The lack of accountability in the nightclub and bar industry in regards to managers and bar owners makes this trend possible. But on the other hand in regards to training & licensing, you have people running government supported nightclub & bar security organizations that have no formal experience in the trade. How can you teach what you have never done. Even if you have expertise in a similar trade does not mean you are qualified to teach or give input. You cannot take a Basic Security Guard course & use it to train bouncers. I am a State of Florida licensed 'D' class security guard instructor and I can tell you that in the USA nightclub and bar security, critical information like ' ID checks, State liquor laws, De-escalation skills & physical intervention are NEVER taught. That's why when a guy comes to me for a job and tells me he's got a 'D' class security license...it don't mean jack shit. That's like taking a jungle guide from Africa and hiring him to help you climb Mt. Everest!!

You can't use a Basic Police Officer training course to train Marine Special Forces. You can't take a Physical Restraint training course from a Prison or Mental Hospital ward and expect it to work in the Nightclub & Bar Security industry. Most people who go to a nightclub or bar are not violent criminals nor are they mentally insane. After three decades in the trade, I have learned that when it comes to use of force, there is no exact science or methodology.

You should not give a violent felon a security license. But then you should not be giving a person who can't speak and/or comprehend the country's language one either. What about an interpreter. Is that interpreter going to be working next to him or her? In de-escalation skills, proper voice control and the ability to speak the common language clear and precise is critical. A thick accent, that can't be understood, will not help calm down an angry, frustrated patron. It will escalate the already bad situation.

SAD

If we allowed people who were scared of guns to become Marine Snipers we could all kiss our asses goodbye. If I have a man who is 92 years old, comes to me wanting to be a trained and certified bouncer, I would say no. Because I know in my heart that this man doesn't have what it takes to do the job. I don't want to waste his time, my time and/or see him get hurt.

If I had no choice but to work with this man on the job, well, I am basically screwed. Not only do I have zero back up but I now have someone I have to protect along with the patrons and staff. In bouncing there is no middle ground, either you are a plus or a minus to the team.

When you have a man who is working with you who you can't understand and he can't understand you. Your security radio is a waste of batteries & worthless. If he is afraid of physical confrontation, you got a double minus!

The only thing that is worse than a bad bouncer is being forced to hire or work with a sad bouncer. They will get you hurt or worse. In the last ten years, what I have witnessed in areas that have mandatory bouncer licensing, the rise of the 'Ninja Bouncer' or 'Mercenary Bouncer'. This is a bouncer or group of bouncers that are hired off the books, dressed in black, no legal affiliation to the club or owners. Hired under the table to 'Remove trouble' . So basically you have jacket fillers at the door all licensed up and standing out front but inside you have the Merc's waiting to take care of business. Sad to say but this type of system that I see on the rise here and abroad will bring rise to a 'Mafia' / 'Thug' type security element.

Ivan 'Doc' Holiday

CHAPTER FIFTEEN

Bouncer the Movie

BOUNCER
AN ACTION FEATURE WRITTEN + DIRECTED BY SAM CLEVELAND

The in development action film BOUNCER brings club life and club bouncers to the big screen. In the film, a bouncer looking to leave behind a life of violence struggles to free himself from a seedy after-dark world of drugs, brutality and corruption.

The film depicts a mix of Hollywood action and true tales gathered by writer and director Sam Cleveland from doorman and bouncers in Australia and from the UK. The Diaries of a Doorman author Stu Armstrong consulted with the writer on the script, providing insights into the lifestyle that become key plot elements in the screenplay. Casting announcements are expected in 2014.

To see a promo trailer and proof-of-concept scene, shot on the nightclub strip of Australia's Gold Coast, visit facebook.com/bouncefilm

Stu has been invited to Australia to play a role in the movie and will also be credited as a script consultant.

Sam Cleveland

The Diaries of a Doorman

Bouncer - Curtis Intro
Dir - Sam Cleveland
Storyboard - Nick Smith

Dolly right across a sea of blurry club movement.

Dolly right to settle on Curtis.

Curtis raises his hand to his earpiece.

Sliver of Curtis' head as he activates earpiece.

Story Board from 'Bouncer the Movie' Kindly Supplied by Sam Cleveland.

CHAPTER SIXTEEN

Channel 4's 'Bouncers'

Bouncers

The response I have had since appearing on Channel 4's documentary 'Bouncers' in November 2013 has been unbelievable for me considering I do not see myself as anything special or great. In my eyes I am just simply a normal bloke, doing his job, who got into working as a bouncer (or doorman as I prefer to call myself) a week after my 18th birthday in 1990. As a kid all during my school days I hated school and youth club discos because of all the noise and rowdiness of all the kids bigger and older than myself, so when I got asked by a work colleague – Russell - to assist him at a private function he was working at I was surprised initially to be asked and even more surprised that I agreed. Russell was a man mountain ex Para who had served in the Falklands, whereas I was a young, tall but thin 18 year old who had on occasions visited the Broadway Nightlife Nightclub in Sudbury, Suffolk and managed to get past the huge doorman without ID.... and this was the very same man asking me to assist him. I was shitting myself, which was a mixture of working as a doorman at that young age, and the fear that sooner or later Russell may discover that I had got past him a few years earlier aged 16 and spent a few nights in the club where he was head doorman. However I recall the night went well and I enjoyed having a few extra quid in my pocket and having girls pay attention to me, I assumed mainly because I was in a suit with a bow tie.

My introduction into working full time as a doorman came after visiting the LA Club in Colchester as a customer and finding an old college friend of mine working there as a doorman. The LA Club was a fairly new club having turned from a snooker hall, and it wasn't long before I was asked to assist and work there with my mate. I was soon working every weekend in a door team of 6-8 doormen who were all of the older breed and who took me under their wing and guided me in the dos and don'ts of working as a doorman in what was becoming a busy club. I feel if I had not worked in this door team for a couple of years then I would not be where I am today in my current full time employment of a Security Industry teacher having completed over 23 years working as a nightclub doorman.

In September 2012 I was asked by the door company I have worked for since 1999 if I could stand in at the Liquor Lounge in Clacton for a night as they were short. I agreed and ventured off to Clacton to do what I believed would be a one off shift. I had previously worked at the Liquor Lounge in the winter of 2009 so I knew the venue and what remained of the management and bar staff. As usual with these things the one night turned into a few weekends as the head doorman at the time had gone into hospital for surgery and was not fit to work, but during my second weekend back there the owner sold the club and a totally new management team were in place along with virtually all new bar staff. With this new ownership also owning another venue in the town, and with most of the door team having previously worked for this owner – and fallen out with them – they all requested to be moved and this left me the longest serving doorman here after only 2 weeks back. Subsequently the phone call came "Ryder… can you be head doorman"? So in what was less than a month I had gone from agreeing to do one night as a stand in to being head doorman and back in the swing of building a door team, getting to know new management and all the customers again.

In October I had a phone call to inform me that a producer from Century Films wanted to meet with me and discuss possible filming of me working as Channel 4 wanted to commission a new series of their 'Bouncers' documentary and what with me being an industry tutor they wanted to focus on me and how I operated. Not one for being shy of a camera having spent 4 years working on Most Haunted's security team I agreed and the producer spent a whole night with me questioning me to gain a knowledge and understanding as to what I was all about. I then heard nothing back from my boss or the producer, however one day a few weeks later I received a phone call to inform me that a camera crew will be following me from the that weekend and that they would be making regular trips down to film me and my team. This gave me all of about 2 days to decide if I wanted to be subject of the national documentary, having always chosen not to watch any documentaries about doormen in the past, so I decided to watch the documentary filmed in Newport and immediately decided that I had to do my part to *try* and raise the image of doorman.

The first night's filming went reasonably ok for me with the exception that I was finding it strange to juggle the 2 roles I suddenly found myself in which was running the door team at a popular club with 400-700 customers in and having a TV crew right up my arse at every turn I made. To be fair to the crew they kept out the way and never got in the way of my work, however it's not every day that whilst working there is a crew standing beside me with an HD camera recording me, a sound man holding a boom to capture the customers conversations and also me having a radio mic on my lapel which picked up everything within a good few meters of me.

The Diaries of a Doorman

So these became the normal working practices every weekend for the best part of 10 months give or take the odd weekend where the crew were off or I was not at work due to my commitment of supporting Southampton Football Club and travelling down to the South Coast for every home game. Due to the constant filming I have become good friends with the director and producer of the show as the camera work did not stop at the club; they followed and filmed me at the boxing gym, my house and in general day to day activities including a whole days SIA Upskilling training. I filmed many hours of footage in my back garden explaining my philosophy of being a doorman, how I like my team to operate, what I thought of my team as individuals, what my family thought of me working and the TV crew even followed my 19 year old son as he took his training and has shown an interest in following in my footsteps and doing a bit of door work. In July 2013 I was asked by my work to relocate for 3 months to Nottingham to take up a teaching position at Hucknall College, and this would result in me having to stop filming and also hand over the reins of the Liquor Lounge to Dan so I filmed my last shift the week before I moved to Nottingham.

After all the filming had finished I remained in constant contact with the director to get the factual side of the documentary correct, and it was then that he started telling me that he was really proud of how the edit was coming along, how I was coming across etc. The problem was the more he told me this the more I started to worry and was convinced that I would come across as a complete wanker and then I started to worry about what had I said, what had I done, how did I look. In hindsight I had nothing to worry about, except the embarrassment of the TV crew waiting to film me as I walked out the bathroom and to my horror it was in the final edit!

When the week arrived that my episode was being aired, I started to feel sick with worry about how would I be received by the public, by door staff across the country who I did not know and more

Stu Armstrong

importantly that in all my 41 years my dear old Mum had never ever heard me swear. I did however constantly post to Facebook and Twitter to inform people that I was on and could they watch me and tell me how I did. For the actual hour the show was live I was in TP's in Colchester with my girlfriend Kim, Julie the manager of the Liquor Lounge and her partner Colin who is the manager of TP's. The nerves were there, more than I had ever experienced standing in front of a full class of students with an external inspector sitting at the back typing away on his laptop and hanging on every word I said and more than being thrust in charge of the Colchester Hippodrome at the age of 22 and being head doorman of a 15 man team most of who were older than me. So to calm the nerves the pints were flowing and not being much of a drinker I was not long until the screen with which my starring role was being shown on was slightly a blur. I did not get to see much of this actual live airing on national TV because by the time the first set of adverts hit the screen my Facebook and Twitter had gone potty.

Facebook from doormen and doorwomen up and down the country suddenly adding me, and Twitter from mostly Southampton Football Club fans who were watching. It's quite surreal and humbling to have people I have never met sending me messages of support and compliments during the show.

Since the show was aired I have had hundreds of personal messages of compliments, I have had email upon email asking for advice, I have had people ringing my work in London asking to attend courses where I will be their teacher but the weirdest part of it all is the being recognised in the street, the shops, the bank, on the train, at the tube station and even the Toby Carvery – where I considered doing a quick toilet check before I decided it was safe for the family to join me!

When I went to see my Mum the following day she was thrilled to have seen her 'little boy' on TV being subject of the documentary and getting his 15 minutes of fame and it was her approval that I was the most happiest with. After a few days I sat down to watch the documentary in a sober state and was pleasantly surprised at how well I came across, I was pleased with how the documentary showed my character to be the calm head doorman who controls his team in an assertive but friendly way. To this day I am still getting feedback, I am still being contacted for training queries and for advice, and I can honestly say I have no regrets over agreeing to be filmed, and I have remained in contact with the director of the show and would jump at the chance to do a follow up if I was asked. If I was to name my one and only regret it would be that my Dad who died in 2006 was not around to join my Mum and see me on the documentary. My Dad would wait up for me every night until I got in from working the door but he would never say anything to me. He would just ask if I was alright and before I had got undressed and in bed his light was off and I could hear his snoring echoing around his room.

I have a big passion for doing our tough job properly in the given circumstances and whereas I have worked all over the UK whether it be 'on the door' or in TV security with Most Haunted I still maintain that there is always someone out there bigger and better than me and that if I and my door team go home safe to their families then I have done my job the best I can. I have not as yet gone back to working on the door as my training commitments take up all my time; however I have been asked to help out for a night so watch this space.

Ryder Scott

CHAPTER 17

So, You want to be a Bouncer?

If you want to join the ranks please Visit
www.safersecurity.com

Owner and senior trainer at Safer Security, Paul Rooks has been working in the private security sector for over 30 years. Paul the senior trainer at Safer Security, has written many of his own courses covering such areas as Self Defence for Doorstaff and unarmed combat for bodyguards along with handcuffing for security operatives.

Pail is a fully qualified, very experienced and fully insured Unarmed Combat Instructor, Close Protection Instructor and Teacher Trainer.

Paul has worked for many years within the UK as a Door Supervisor and Bodyguard and has also had extensive experience in Eastern Africa in such countries as Kenya, Uganda and Tanzania, since 1994.

Paul also works as a Security Consultant assisting people managing their events and running their training contracts. Paul has an extensive history working in frontline Door Supervision and as a Bodyguard, this was many years before the SIA licence system came in to operation but he also has embraced all SIA training and activities and studied to gain all of the modern qualifications needed to run an approved awarding body centre and to instruct to the SIA and Award body standards.

So you want to be a Bouncer? Then do it………
With Safer Security **www.safersecurity.com**

Knives not Lives

After meeting Steve Cairney and becoming friends at some BBAD Bare Knuckle Boxing events and hearing the tragic story of Leon his son, I am a huge supporter of his campaign for awareness.
Being a father to three sons brought this home all the more to me, and also working as a doorman I have faced issues in regard to knife crime on a number of occasions. When I was made aware of Steve's campaign I knew that I had to try and help. If by having Leon's story in all of my books just one life saved then it is more than worth it. Knife crime is all to prevalent in this day and age and people don't stand up and be counted, Steve is standing up to be counted, and both now and in the future I will be there to support Steve in his courageous campaign.

Choose Live, Not Knives!

Stu Armstrong

Stu Armstrong

Choose Live, Not Knives!

My Son, Leon came out of school at the age of 15 and enrolled with the army at the age of 16, determined to make difference in the World. He did tours in both Afghanistan, Bosnia, Ireland and was a keen boxer who represented the army and got in to the finals in Germany. He came out of the army when he was twenty, due to losing one of his army pals in a road side bomb.

Once he came out the army he started to work with his dad, within demolition and progressed well within this new career path. He had just started a young family and had two little girls (The girls now are at the age of five and three). Leon had worked with dad for the past five years and was a very happy, positive young man and a lot going for him.

On the 22nd December 2012 when Leon was at twenty five years old, my wife and I were called at around 2.30am by a person at the door who mentioned that he thought that Leon had been stabbed. I got dressed and told my wife that everything would be OK and ran down the street and into a back garden, where someone was trying to resuscitate Leon.

I pushed him out of the way and fell to my knees and picked my son up in my arms and eyes where as bright as stars and body as cold as ice and told him he would be OK, because his dad was here. The knife was still stuck in Leon. The next thing, the emergency services where there but Leo was pronounced dead at the scene.

A few days later we had to identify the body and we had to wait two months to bury him. The whole family was torn apart. It has only been the last few months until we have been able to restart building our lives.

We would not want any family to go through this. **NO PARENT SHOULD EVER HAVE TO BURY THERE OWN CHILD.**

CHOOSE LIFE NOT KNIVES.

A big thank you to Stu Armstrong for all his support and raising awareness to others via our sad loss and story, If we could stop one family going through this heart ache, nightmare and grief, then the above made a difference.

Rest in peace oor son Leon Cairney!!!

Stephen Cairney

ABOUT THE AUTHOR

Stu Armstrong first of all is a loving a proud father of his three amazing sons, by day he is an Implementation Consultant, by night he is a Doorman with 19 years of experience. From a very early age Stu has loved books and been fascinated by words and the power of the written word, an ambition has always been to write a book.

Stu's first book, The Diaries of a Doorman, was written & self-published in December 2013, with a zero budget and he was lucky enough to have some very good friends who helped him with artwork, proofreading and Stu's oldest son helped with the photography.

The Diaries of a Doorman - A collection of true short stories will be followed up with more tiles in 2014.

Since the original publication Stu Armstrong has announced that by sheer public demand and the amazing sales and reviews of his first book 'The Diaries of a Doorman – A Collection of True Short Stories' that a follow up 'The Diaries of a Doorman Volume 2 – Bouncers & Bravado' will be out in spring 2014.

Me and the Lads looking after JLS at a book signing

For more information about the Author Stu Armstrong please visit www.facebook.com/stuarmstrongauthor

The Diaries of a Doorman

Out Spring 2014
www.facebook.com/bookdoorman
www.facebook.com/stuarmstrongauthor
www.ukbouncers.com

Printed in Germany
by Amazon Distribution
GmbH, Leipzig